**BLACK
LIFE
MATTER**

**BLACK
LIFE
MATTER**
BLACKNESS,
RELIGION,
AND THE
SUBJECT

**BIKO
MANDELA
GRAY**

DUKE UNIVERSITY PRESS

Durham and London   2022

BLACKNESS, RELIGION, AND THE SUBJECT

BIKO

MANDELA

© 2022 DUKE UNIVERSITY PRESS. All rights reserved
Printed in the United States of America on acid-free paper ∞
Designed by Courtney Leigh Richardson
Typeset in Minion Pro and Degular
by Westchester Publishing Services

Library of Congress Cataloging-in-Publication Data
Names: Gray, Biko Mandela, author.
Title: Black life matter : blackness, religion, and the subject / Biko
Mandela Gray.
Description: Durham : Duke University Press, 2022. | Includes
bibliographical references and index.
Identifiers: LCCN 2022003205 (print)
LCCN 2022003206 (ebook)
ISBN 9781478013907 (hardcover)
ISBN 9781478014843 (paperback)
ISBN 9781478022114 (ebook)
Subjects: LCSH: Racism—United States. | Racism—United States—
Philosophy. | Black lives matter movement. | Racism in law
enforcement—United States. | Racism against Black people—
United States. | Police murders—United States. | Murder
victims—United States. | Police brutality—United States. | African
Americans—Social conditions. | United States—Race relations—
History. | BISAC: SOCIAL SCIENCE / Black Studies (Global) |
RELIGION / Philosophy
Classification: LCC E185.615 .G671825 2022 (print) |
LCC E185.615 (ebook) | DDC 305.800973—dc23/eng/20220509
LC record available at https://lccn.loc.gov/2022003205
LC ebook record available at https://lccn.loc.gov/2022003206

For Andrea

And for Aiyana, Tamir,
Alton, Sandra, Jordan,

and all the black lives lost
to state-sanctioned violence,

and their families

Contents

Acknowledgments

"Here, in this here place": these were Baby Suggs's first recorded words in the Clearing. I want to thank those who have made "this here place" possible. And I want to apologize in advance to those whom I may have forgotten.

I want to thank the readers from Duke University Press for their careful suggestions and thoughtful critiques. I have tried to incorporate much of what you all suggested in this text, and I hope *Black Life Matter* reflects that engagement. I also have to thank Marquis Bey for reading an early draft of chapter 2; I think you said it best when you called my work para-academic— you liberated me in ways I still cannot articulate. And I must give the biggest thanks to Sandra Korn, my editor, for showing faith in this project from the outset. We've come a long way from the booth at AAR; you are the best editor this young scholar could ask for.

I presented earlier drafts of this text at different places. And I am so thankful for those who invited me to share my thoughts—people who have become friends: thank you to Ryan Johnson, Dustin Atlas, Sharday Mosurinjohn, Amarnath Amarasingham, Shobhana Xavier, and Adriaan Van Klinken. It is a profound gift to know each of you.

I am so thankful for my teachers and professors who trained me and offered support and wisdom along the way: Bill Parsons, Marcia Brennan, James Faubion, Steven Crowell, James Sidbury, and Lewis Gordon. Elias Bongmba has been a caring teacher; he also gave me my Levinas and sharpened my phenomenological sensibilities. And Jeff Kripal has been there for me all along, encouraging me to be fearless in my thinking and giving me counsel when I needed it. I must also thank my former peers and newer students from graduate school for their constant collegiality and friendship: Christopher Driscoll, Monica Miller, Justine Bakker, Nathanael Homewood, Rachel Schneider,

Shardé Chapman, David Kline, Mark DeYoung, DeAnna Daniels, and Hasan Henderson-Lott. And I would be remiss if I didn't acknowledge Courtney Bryant, whose friendship, collegiality, and fierce engagement with me on flesh have only helped to sharpen the ethical dimensions of my thinking.

I am thankful to those who have been mentors for me: Fr. Phillip Linden and Victor Anderson made and make me a better thinker and stronger philosopher, encouraging me to do what I didn't think I could. Anthony Pinn was my fiercest interlocutor in the study of black religion at Rice; thank you for your laughter, your rigor, your brilliance, and your time. Stephen Finley saw in me what I could not see in myself; I'm not sure I would have made it this far without your encouragement and guidance, and I still look up to you.

A massive thank you goes to Christina Sharpe, whose work and person demonstrate the care about which she writes. This text would not be what it is without you. Thank you—for your time, your encouragement, your care.

I was lucky enough to be hired by the religion department at Syracuse University, where much of this book was drafted. To Jim Watts, Gail Hamner, Zak Braiterman, and the Department of Religion: thank you for your collegiality, support, and guidance. A special thanks goes to Virginia Burrus and Marcia Robinson, who, each in their own way, flesh out the possibilities that intellectual rigor and compassionate friendship can occasion.

I must also thank my students at Syracuse—graduate and undergraduate—who were gracious enough to let me be a part of their lives. Thank you to my graduate students who sharpened my ideas and my teaching: Danae Faulk, Rachel Carpenter, Blake Garland-Tirado, Aarti Patel, Jordan Loewen, and Sarah Nahar. And thank you to my undergraduates who never stopped challenging me and continually made teaching more than worthwhile: Volda, Pat, Tayla, Jake, Dominique, Sonia, Breanna, Kayla, KJ, Tim, Vishwas, Ericka, and Bekkah. You know who you are, and I am so proud of each of you.

Since I've been at Syracuse, I've made some new and dear friends: Chris Eng, Susan Thomas, Terrell Winder, Linda Zhang, and Jenn Jackson. Each of you have sat with me, laughed with me, sometimes cried with me; each of you have held me up in ways I cannot quantify. Thank you for the texts and the calls, the dinners and the UNO games, the invitations to teach and express my aesthetic sensibilities. Each of you know what you mean to me, and if you don't, I'll say it here: I have nothing but love for each of you.

To William Robert, my beloved William: I do not have words for who you are to me, so I will say this: The effort must be total if the results are to be effective.

There are families you're born into and families you choose. Secunda Joseph (my Ida B. Wells), Carie Cauley (your prayers have sustained me), Rhys Caraway (my fierce and courageous little brother), Cleve Tinsley (my visionary older brother), Lanecia Rouse-Tinsley (my lodestar and muse for what it means to do this work in love and compassion), Malik and Jinaki Muhammad (my power couple), Stevens Orozco (my daredevil—you know what that means), and Janet Baker (my Baby Suggs) are comrades who have become more than friends. I wouldn't have it any other way.

Doing life together is neither easy nor simple. It is a praxis, cultivated over time and sharpened through joy and sorrow. I'm so thankful that these folks have chosen to do life with me: Jessica Davenport has sat with me, laughed with me, cried with me, prayed with me, listened to me, and thought with me in ways I cannot fully convey; Brandi Holmes is a gift of strength, humor, joy, prayer, and beauty—you are a gem of a person, my gem; Yolanda Archibald has been my refuge of joy, laughter, tenacity, and care; Ashleigh Bing, you are my resting place, my fiercest teacher on integrity and authenticity; Edward Stephens III, I didn't think brotherhood could extend beyond biological family before you, but you've now made me a believer; and Jason Jeffries is the older brother this oldest child didn't know he needed but is so happy to have. When I say I love each of you, I mean it.

To Niki Kasumi Clements: I cannot stress how much you mean to me. Everyone gets an advisor in graduate school, but you are more than that. You helped me make a mosaic out of broken pieces. You are my teacher. And I will always be your student. I love you.

To my family—to Mom and Pops, to Rechab, Brittany, Aaron, Zipporah, Jonathan, Hadassah, Veronica, and Dakota; to my grandmothers—"Mama" Annie Mae and "Ma-Ma" Clara; to Mom and Pops Sawyer, to Vincent and Aunt Tricia, and to my two other grandmothers—Mama Annie Johnson and Mama Ruby (may you both rest in all the peace and power you deserve): all I can say is *I love you*. To say any more would be reductive and damaging to who you each are to me.

And last, to the one to whom this book is dedicated, to Andrea, my partner, my best friend, my lover, my confidant, my refuge, my solace, my peace, my joy, my heart, the one in whom I live, move, and have my being, the one who reminds me that all things are possible, the one who is my living proof of God's existence, the one in whom I find hope: there is love, and there is *Love*. And then there is *You*.

INTRODUCTION

FOUR BLACK LIVES

I had to take care.—Christina Sharpe, *In the Wake*

She was seven years old. And she was adorable. In one of her pictures, she is smiling. Behind her are three Disney princesses: Sleeping Beauty, Cinderella, and the Little Mermaid. She must have really liked those princesses, too; she liked to sleep under a blanket adorned by one of them. (Her grandmother, Mertilla, once told me and a beloved of mine which one, but I can't remember now. And it's this lack of memory that haunts me.[1]) Maybe, sometimes, she dreamed of being a princess. Perhaps her dreams were filled with music. Maybe they were Disney musicals. I only hope that they weren't nightmares.

Mertilla told us that Aiyana was sleeping under the princess blanket when the cops came. Mertilla had fallen asleep on the couch with her.

But then the flash-bang came in. Startled, Mertilla fell off the couch. A man walked in, turned to the right, and shot her, Aiyana Stanley-Jones, a little black girl, in her sleep. While she dreamed.

I really hope she wasn't having a nightmare.

* * *

He was twelve. And by all accounts, he was a clown; he loved to make people laugh. He was playful, too; like most kids, he had an active imagination. One day, at the community center near where he lived, he traded his mom's cell phone for his friend's toy gun. But you know how kids do; playtime is rough. The toy had lost some of its parts. The orange cap had fallen off, and now this toy gun looked more realistic.

Tamir didn't mind, though. Imagination has neither time nor patience for perfection. You make do with what you have: a tree can become a fortress; a gazebo, a vantage point for finding the bad guys. I like to think that he was after bad guys that day; he'd point the toy here and there, keeping them at bay. He was a kid, playing with a toy.

When they drove up, however, they didn't see a kid playing with a toy. They saw something else. And they asked no questions; they weren't going to wait for answers. They were out for blood; in their minds, *Tamir* was a bad guy. One of them shot. Twice.

Tamir would not survive.

* * *

He was thirty-seven. Life hadn't always been good to him, either. He'd been in trouble with the law from time to time. But things were changing. He loved music, and he realized he could make part of his living from sharing it with others. He'd made friends with an owner of a convenience store, and they'd agreed that he could sell CDs on a table out front.

I don't know how much money he made, but perhaps it wasn't only about profits. After all, he didn't simply sell the CDs; he also played music while he sold them—so much so that "if you didn't hear music, he wasn't there."[2] After a while, people started calling him the CD Man. It had a nice ring to it: Alton Sterling, the CD Man. He let it stick.

But one night, somebody kept harassing him. He flashed a revolver in his pocket and told the person to leave him alone. The heckler made a call, and they came.

When they arrived, they were aggressive and unrelenting. But it wasn't clear why they were there—let alone why they were being aggressive toward *him*.

"What I do?" he said. No answer: they'd found their suspect, and they weren't going to dignify him with a response. They pinned him down. And then they saw the pistol in his pocket.

There are no CDs—or a CD man—in front of the Triple S Mart in Baton Rouge anymore.

* * *

She was twenty-eight. And she loved the babies. In fact, she wanted one. She'd gotten pregnant before, but the baby didn't come to term. This took a toll on her. But if she couldn't have one of her own, she would do her best to make sure that all the children she knew were loved. She started making videos. She did fundraisers for children's sports. Things had been hard, but love was what got her through.

And things were looking up. She'd gotten a new job—at her alma mater, of all places. Maybe that's what she was thinking about when she was driving that day—all the possibilities. And that day was a good day for a drive; the sun was out, and it was warm. But then a car started tailing her. It was a state trooper, and it clearly had somewhere to be. She tried to move out of its way; she switched lanes. But she didn't signal.

The lights came on. When she stopped, he got out and told her she didn't signal when she switched lanes. She was incredulous. And she let him know it.

While he wrote the ticket, Sandy lit a cigarette. The trooper returned and told her to put it out. She told him no. And that was it.

Three days later, Sandra Bland would be found dead in her jail cell.

* * *

Aiyana Stanley-Jones. Tamir Rice. Alton Sterling. Sandra Bland. This book is about these four lives. It's about how these four lives matter.

Black Lives Matter. For many, the phrase is as aspirational as it is declarative. We claim—we scream, we shout, we declare—*black lives matter* because it appears they don't; too many of us have come to know Aiyana, Tamir, Alton, and Sandra through their deaths. They have become ancestors in the worst way; they appear to us in the very moments in which they disappear. Lost to us in the very moment we know who they are, we are confronted with the question: Do black lives actually matter?

Appearances can be deceiving, though. It is precisely this structure of dis/appearance that discloses how Aiyana, Tamir, Alton, and Sandra are still with us. They still speak. In speaking, they still matter—to those who love and cared for them, and yes, to those who have no patience for them. In sitting with these four lives, we come to recognize that black lives matter to this world—even to those who would claim otherwise, even to those who killed them.

In this book, I call those people normative subjects. *Black Life Matter* argues that the normative subjects of this world are sustained by the symbolic, physical, philosophical, and religious violence they enact against black life, against black lives. This requires sitting with the lives stolen by these very normative subjects; it requires attending to those lives that, for many, no longer register in our collective consciousness. In sitting with them, we find resources to criticize the violence at the heart of normative subject formation—a violence that is, as I hope to show, helplessly and relentlessly antiblack.

Norms hide themselves. (That's what makes them norms.) Because of this, I leave the subject undefined. I don't racialize it. I don't tether it to a specific gender. I also leave questions of class, sexuality, and nationality open. In fact, after this, I will rarely use the word *normative* to describe them—I'll just call them subjects. In doing this, I am adopting and criticizing the philosophy of the subject—particularly Martin Heidegger's conception. Heidegger told his readers that "subjectivity" could be best captured in what he called the "they" or the "one" (*Das Man*).[3] *Das Man* is the everyday way in which *Dasein* engages with the world and others in it. *Dasein* moves as one does; it speaks as one would speak. It acts in accordance with what one would understand as normative, acceptable, and sanctioned modes of conduct.[4] Subjects, then, are those who live from and reinforce the norms of this world.

Black Life Matter criticizes this structure of subjecthood and its violence, arguing that black death founds and justifies normative subjecthood. It does so by exposing the cops who excessively, reactively, and violently brutalized and killed their victims. In this text, cops are the primary examples of normative subjects; police have demonstrated that they are incapable of anything other than violence—particularly violence against black lives.

Cops, however, aren't the only normative subjects. If subjects live from and reinforce the norms of this world, then subjects are also those who *rely upon* cops to keep order. Subjects shudder at the idea of abolishing the police; they claim that all cops aren't bad; they might even offer explicit support for police, claiming that *blue lives matter*—even as they claim they aren't racist. This is the case because, as I will say later, subjects privilege their own perspectives more than anything or anyone else; they think their perspectives take primacy over others, and anything or anyone that challenges this primacy will suffer the consequences.

Black Life Matter therefore argues that cops are proxies for a structure of subjecthood that is compelled to enact cognitive, symbolic, religious, and philosophical violence when it is confronted with the indeterminate movement and presence of blackness. And it is precisely this subjective compulsion that discloses how important black life—or, more precisely, the killing, maiming, violating, exploiting, and brutalizing of black life—is to normative subjects. Without enacting violence against us, normative subjects would cease to exist.

After sitting with these lives, I am fully convinced that the police need to be abolished. The institution that is the police conditions the subjects that engage in (and justify) lethal and brutal antiblack violence, and because of this, it has lost any ethical purchase, especially when it comes to black life. In this regard, this text could be understood as clearing philosophical ground to make a case for abolition as an ethical stance from the perspective of philosophy of religion. While this text doesn't outline specific calls for police abolition, the chapters nevertheless describe the conditions of antiblack violence that, I hope, will encourage readers to adopt, or at least consider, police abolition as an ethical stance.

Black Life Matter isn't only about the violence, however. It gestures toward the capacity for life in the midst of what Christina Sharpe might call the "requirement for our death." In this way, this book is a work of care—for the dead. And this kind of care, Sharpe intimates, "means work." It is "hard emotional, physical, and intellectual work that demands vigilant attendance to the needs of the dying, to ease their way, and also to the needs of the living."[5] Sharpe calls this kind of work "wake work." She describes wake work as "a mode of inhabiting *and* rupturing this episteme with our known lived and un/imaginable lives. With that analytic we might imagine otherwise from what we know *now* in the wake of slavery."[6]

This book is my way of enacting wake work. Sitting with Aiyana, Tamir, Alton, and Sandra does not simply expose the violence of normative subject formation; it also seeks to rupture this violence by "imagining otherwise," by demonstrating how black lives still speak from beyond the grave. We who live in the wake of these deaths are still here, and our being here produces a radical ethical demand to care—for the living and for the dead, for those who are struggling under the violence of antiblackness now as well as those who were killed by it. *Black Life Matter* is therefore my attempt to "attend to, care for, comfort, and defend those already dead, those dying, and those living lives consigned to the possibility of always-imminent death, life lived in the presence of death."[7]

While this world has moved on, I believe it is necessary to defend the dead. Aiyana, Tamir, Alton, Sandra, and so many others were not mere tragedies.

They lived. They led lives. The fact that their lives were stolen (or the fact that this world continues to justify this theft through its advocacy of police) should only call us to stay with them, to not move on, to wrestle and reckon with the power and promise of their lives and legacies. And, like Sharpe said, that requires work—the hard, painful, yet necessary work of care.

Philosophical Eulogy as Care

Care isn't a cheap sentimental term. *I don't care* and *you don't care* are far harsher than they seem at first glance. After all, affects like anger or even hatred signal investment.[8] But apathy? Apathy doesn't give a damn. It is a disposition of utter disregard.

When it comes to these lives, it's easy to become apathetic. It's easy to move on. Aiyana was murdered in 2010; Tamir in 2014. Sandra Bland died in 2015, and Sterling was gunned down in 2016. By the time this book appears, many years will have passed since their names were in the headlines. Now, if they do appear, it's on the anniversaries of their deaths, or when yet another black person is murdered by the state. The cops kill so much that it's hard to keep track. So, you shed a tear, post something via social media, and move on. Or conversely—and on a wider scale—you draft a vapid piece of legislation, make a speech, "celebrate" or "bring awareness to" something, and move on. Once you've done your piece, the life no longer matters. You've become apathetic. That is, until the next black life is killed. And then you rinse and repeat. But in the end, you don't care.

Black Life Matter refuses to move on. In fact, central to this book's method is a commitment to stay (I'll say more about this in just a bit), to not move on—because moving on is precisely what subjects do. Subjects don't stay. They don't remember or defend the dead. In fact, they might even justify why the dead had to die. They gather what they need from a life and then move on. They don't care.

Sharpe wants to "think care as a problem for thought," and perhaps this is the case because care discloses the problems *of* thought.[9] *Black Life Matter*, then, takes up the problematic of care by enacting philosophical eulogy; this text is a collection of stories about the dead that have philosophical and ethical importance.[10] These stories include phenomenology, affect studies, black critical theory, and philosophical ethics, and they do so in service of speaking (back) to philosophy of religion. *Black Life Matter* is therefore a sustained criticism of the religious logics and structures of thinking—theodicy (chapter 1), ontotheology and interpellation (chapter 2), and affect and religious experience (chapter 3)—that inform, enable, and sustain subjects in their enactments of black death and antiblack violence.

These stories are as painful as they are critical. But they are, and remain, eulogies. They are, and they remain, good words about the lives we've lost. I give these eulogies because there is also something else, something otherwise, something beyond what those logics can contain or even fathom. Even in their absence, Aiyana, Tamir, Alton, and Sandra—among so many others—live on. They live as afterlives.[11] There is something about Aiyana's, Tamir's, Alton's, and Sandra's lives that "survive[s] this insistent Black exclusion, this ontological negation" that occasioned their deaths.[12]

Those who have died—those who were murdered—are no longer with us. They are now our ancestors. That cannot be overcome. And it certainly cannot be overlooked. But—*but*—we can honor the dead by turning to them, sitting with them, caring for them, and therefore allowing them to form, disform, and inform us. This process of in/dis/forming renders the finality of death a farce. Death isn't the final word. It never has been. It never will be.

This book therefore highlights a modality of life—by which I mean a mode of feeling, moving, connecting, and relating—that runs counter to the death-dealing structures of this world. And it does so by listening to what stolen black lives still have to say. In listening, this book declares that black lives matter—to us, to the world, to the world's subjects. In making this declaration, *Black Life Matter* calls us to care for black lives. And care is so much more than sentiment. It is a requirement. It requires that we stay with the lives.

It requires that we *sit with* them.

Sitting-With

I've been trying to articulate a method of encountering a past that is not past. A method along the lines of a sitting with, a gathering, and a tracking of phenomena that disproportionately and devastatingly affect Black peoples any and everywhere we are.—Christina Sharpe, *In the Wake*

I use the phrase *sit with* intentionally and technically. *Sitting-with* is my method. It is the way I handle the lives and deaths at the heart of this book.

Sitting with someone is an act of care.[13] If you've ever sat with someone, you know that they are your focus.[14] You aren't distracted easily—if at all. You might cry with them as they mourn; you might call the medical staff to come ease their pain, or you might administer medicine yourself. A beloved might call you: "Do you have a minute? I need to talk." It doesn't matter if you do or don't—you respond. You tell them you're on the way, or you sit with them on the phone as they share what they've been dealing with.

Sometimes, the situation calls you to speak, to share your thoughts. Other times, your presence itself is enough; words would only do more damage.[15] No matter the specifics, you're called to respond, to be there, to show up. When you sit with someone, you respond to them. You tend to them. You attend to them.

Sitting with someone isn't always easy. Especially when they are struggling—and even more so when this struggle is one of life and death. In these moments, it is hard to stay there; as your beloved cries or sits in shock, as they bleed or are afraid, as they face their death, you might find yourself wanting to leave. You want to look away. But you don't. You stay. For as long as you can. For them. As a method, sitting-with begins with a commitment to not move on.

This book makes that methodological commitment. It doesn't move on. Each chapter will have moments that are hard to read. They were excruciatingly hard to write. In writing this book, I have listened to police interviews; I have read newspaper articles and after-action reports; I have read testimonies. And yes, I have watched videos when they were available—multiple times.

In doing all this, I am struck by how I am never desensitized, how the brutality continues to make me shudder and bring me to tears. I am struck by how the abject disregard for black life—which is to say, human life (even if that term *human* means little when it comes to black life)—wears on my psyche, takes a toll on my soul.[16] I wrote this text because I haven't moved on, because sitting-with requires the sometimes painful commitment to remain and remember.

This commitment is also risky. There are ethical difficulties with reproducing narratives of antiblack violence. Narrating the violence as I do here risks becoming trauma porn. Saidiya Hartman once said as much:

> Rather than inciting indignation, too often [stories of antiblack violence] immure us to pain by virtue of their familiarity . . . and especially because they reinforce the spectacular character of black suffering. What interests me are the ways we are called upon to participate in such scenes. Are we witnesses who confirm the truth of what happened in the face of the world-destroying capacities

of pain, the distortions of torture, the sheer unrepresentability of terror, and the repression of the dominant accounts? Or are we voyeurs fascinated with and repelled by exhibitions of terror and sufferance? . . . At issue here is the precariousness of empathy and the uncertain line between witness and spectator.[17]

Telling these stories runs the risk of crossing "the uncertain line between witness and spectator." This is what institutions, corporations, politicians, and celebrities do, after all: they know that "the exposure of the mutilated body yield[s]" massive profits.[18]

There are other related risks, too. It is possible for some viewers to receive pleasure from watching, even if this pleasure comes in the form of repulsion. They might watch these videos or hear these stories and feel good about feeling bad. For these people, watching is a form of catharsis: their feelings about these scenes—whether it be anger, sadness, or so-called outrage—cleanses their consciences; it confirms for them that they are good people. In the end, they enjoy what they see. And the very possibility of enjoyment is precisely what prompts Hartman to raise questions.[19]

I hear Hartman; I am moved by her work. But I wonder, along with Fred Moten, if not telling these stories actually hinders this world from finding enjoyment in spectacles of antiblack violence.[20] This world finds enjoyment in black suffering, and it would seem that this structure of enjoyment cannot be fully overcome—that's one of the insights of Hartman's analysis. Is there a way, then, to expose, disrupt, and undo this perverse violence of enjoyment? Are there ways to become witnesses and not spectators? Or, as Moten puts it, "is there a way to subject this unavoidable model of subjection to a radical breakdown?"[21]

I offer sitting-with as a possible way. In remaining witnesses, we stay with the stories. We stay with the lives. When you sit with someone, you worry about them; you are concerned for *them*. As your beloved cries or sleeps, you are angered, upset, by the fact of their pain. You might worry about the doctors and their medical standards; you might be angry that the doctors missed a diagnosis or failed to provide adequate treatment. And that anger points you to the structures or the conditions that continue to produce the pain they experience.

In all of this, you don't try to explain or justify—to them, to yourself— why or how they suffer. You don't abstract away from their experience; you don't fashion a theory out of their pain. You stay with them, holding them if you can, and wondering what you can do to try and change the situation.

Sitting with these lives, then, requires that we commit to staying, to not moving on, and that we do not abstract away from them. These lives aren't materials for making theory. They instead point us toward the violence of making theory, toward the violence of making abstractions, which is to say, sitting with these lives and deaths means we behold them *in their opacity*.[22] Aiyana, Tamir, Alton, and Sandra aren't fully available to us. They are not examples—they are synecdoches. They hold so much more than we can fathom. And because of this, we do not try to discern their motivations or produce general principles from their lives. Sitting with them in this way might make it possible to radically break down and maybe even break through the violence of spectatorship.

This is why I have reproduced these stories. I didn't write this book to exploit these lives.[23] I wrote it because these lives called to me, because they prompted me to turn my analytic and philosophical lenses to criticize the nature of subjects and the attendant philosophical structures that enable and justify them in their pursuit and enactments of antiblack violence. I am able to do this only because I sit with the *lives*; the subject and its thinking are my targets of criticism, but only because the lives point me there. Sitting-with requires that we don't move on. It requires that we stay. That's this method's first step. It is also its primary commitment.

Sitting-With as Paraphenomenology

What if the thing sustains itself in that absence or eclipse of meaning that withholds from the thing the horrific honorific of object? At the same time, what if the value of that absence or excess is given to us only in and by way of a kind of failure or inadequacy—or perhaps more precisely, by way of a history of exclusion, serial expulsion, presence's ongoing taking of leave—so that the non-attainment of meaning or ontology, of source or origin, is the only way to approach the thing in its informal . . . material totality?—Fred Moten, "The Case of Blackness"

[Husserl's] abstraction permits a "philosophical" forgetfulness of just how fundamental the deracination of personhood is to the constitution of human society in modernity.—R. A. Judy, *Sentient Flesh*

This part will be technical.[24]

Black Life Matter sits with these lives in a particular way. It describes the encounters between the lives and the police officers who occasioned their demise. And it does so in service of disclosing the philosophical and theoretical structures and logics that condition the violence normative subjects enact in service of securing the meaning of their existence. Sitting-with, then, is a mode of critical philosophical description.

If *critical philosophical description* feels phenomenological in its phrasing, that's because it is—kind of. Sitting-with draws its inspiration from phenomenology, but it doesn't adhere to the strictures of classical phenomenological methodology, particularly its preoccupation with first-person description. Phenomenology may turn to "the things themselves," but, eventually, it turns away from those things; it turns back toward itself. Bracketing (*epoché*) the existence of the world and its objects, classical phenomenology turns to the things themselves only to turn back to the subject of experience. Once the brackets are put in place, phenomenology invests in the experiencer, not the experienced.[25]

> The *epoché* can also be said to be the radical and universal method by which I apprehend myself purely: as Ego, and with my own pure conscious life, in and by which the entire Objective world exists for me and is precisely as it is for me. Anything belonging to the world, any spatiotemporal being, exists for me—that is to say, is accepted by me—in that I experience it, perceive it, remember it, think of it somehow, judge about it, value it, desire it, or the like. . . . By my living, by my experiencing, thinking, valuing, and acting, I can enter no world other than the one that gets its sense and acceptance or status in and from me, myself.[26]

Brackets center the experiencing subject. They focus the subject's attention on its own modes of thinking and understanding; brackets are (erected as) philosophical blinders. It isn't simply that phenomenology starts and ends with experiencing subjects—the very mode of description is situated within the subject's perspective. With the brackets firmly in place, the subject is free to interrogate their own ways of engaging and understanding the world. In so doing, brackets deceive the subject into thinking it is at the center of the world it experiences. In the end, classical phenomenological methodology is, well, *self*-serving.

But good phenomenologists know that the brackets are an artifice. Erecting them may bring clarity. It might even bring a certain kind of critical self-reflexivity.[27] But at the end of the day, the brackets are about the subject; they withhold access to the very material world with which subjects must reckon and wrestle. And that material world, that world of matter—of what I'll later call flesh—cannot be dismissed.

To account for this, certain phenomenologists draw a distinction between what we might call *encounters* with matter that do not yet have meaning (I'll have more to say about this later in this introduction and throughout the book) and the meaningful *experiences* that draw from matter to make sense; you know, or at least have an idea of, what you're experiencing.[28] Experiences are, phenomenologically speaking, more than encounters. They require a relationship between you, what you're encountering, and the structures of signification that give this perception meaning. Turning to what is experienced only to turn away from it, phenomenological methodology doesn't take care. It moves on.

But what if we didn't turn away? What if, instead of staying with experiencing subjects, we stayed with *what is experienced*? What if we described *encounters*, following them where they lead us? We wouldn't yet be dealing with objects, but instead recognizing how the production of the object is a violent affair. What was once an object would show itself as something else, something beyond the constraints of the "horrific honorific of object," something that would exceed the constraints of signifying subjects whose signifying cognitions reduce plentiful matter into intelligible entities.

From that perspective, we would begin to catch, but only catch, glimpses of something that the subject can't apprehend and arrest in its first-person perspective, something that "is tantamount to another, fugitive, sublimity altogether."[29] Catching that glimpse would be enough to expose the subject, showing that its own claim to primacy is nothing other than a violent artifice of its own making. It would show that intentionality isn't directed but circular, coming from and returning to the experiencing subject. And it would show that this circularity is a necessary and enabling condition for all kinds of symbolic and physical violence.

Turning to encounters instead of experiences changes and exposes things; it remembers that the phenomenological brackets are an artifice; it recognizes that the very constitution of the subject depends upon the hermeneutic and physical violence subjects enact. Turning to encounters allows us to sidestep the "'philosophical' forgetfulness of just how fundamental the deracination of personhood is to the constitution of human society in modernity."

I call this approach *paraphenomenology*, and I offer it in service of attending to and caring for those who were taken from us. Paraphenomenology takes us elsewhere; it attends to—it *sits with*—the lives that were stolen not as objects of analysis, but instead as living matter that exceeds the significations of the subjects who encountered and then enacted violence against them. In so doing, it disrupts the desire for coherence at the heart of phenomenological analysis (as well as much of philosophical analysis more generally), calling into question the assumptive privileging of the first-person perspective as a surefire way of understanding life and its possibilities. Paraphenomenology sits with black lives that were taken from us as an act of care; it is a mode of wake work; it is my way of defending the dead in the name of life. Black life.

PARAPHENOMENOLOGY AS PHILOSOPHICAL CRITIQUE

Paraphenomenology stays with the lives that were stolen so that we might catch that glimpse of their irreducible indeterminacy. In catching that glimpse, we wouldn't be able to explain what we encountered; we would simply behold this indeterminacy in its irreducibility, allowing it to guide us and take us to the structures that have set upon it. When you sit with someone, *they* guide your perspective. They take primacy—not you.

Sitting with these black lives, then, does not allow us to affirm the phenomenological method; they expose its problems and its violence. They expose how the first-person perspective is the way the subject privileges itself; they show that this very privileging is not simply limited to the subjects who enact it—which is to say, these lives show how the privileging of the first-person perspective is embedded in, and the enabling condition for, the very institutions that sanction, tolerate, encourage, and justify even more violence.

The officers I discuss in this book live into and express a structure of subjectivity that privileges the first-person perspective, and they do so because they are called, sanctioned, encouraged, and justified by this very privilege. Officers constitute their victims—as bodies (chapter 1), as threats (chapter 2), as resistant and affectively resonant objects (chapter 3)—by reducing their encounters with irreducibly living, moving, feeling, and loving black flesh into intentional experiences of meanings they could understand, apprehend, constrain, and, in many cases, kill. And they do so in the name of larger institutional structures that embrace the phenomenological privileging of the first-person perspective.[30] If cops are extreme examples of the violence of the subject, it is only because they are sanctioned by other subjects to do so.

The Supreme Court case *Graham v. Connor* is an example of this: in adjudicating a case of police brutality, the court ruled that "the 'reasonableness' of a particular use of force must be judged from *the perspective of a reasonable officer on the scene*."[31] The law itself therefore privileges the reductions, constitutions, and intentional (which, again, means directed) experiences of the officers who kill; the officers—the subjects—in these encounters are the only ones deemed reasonable, and, as I say later in this introduction, it is precisely this capacity for reason, for thinking, that sediments the primacy of the officers' perspective.

Let me be clear: I do not arrive at these conclusions because I hate cops. Hate requires investment, and I am not invested enough in cops to hate them. The implicit call for abolition that motivates this book comes from a love for black life, not from a hatred for police. I do not propose reforms or call for individual cops' executions. I do not seek to change policing in this country; I seek to *expose* it and those who support it. In so doing, I hope this book will push others to recognize the violence inherent in policing, and push for something else. Sitting with these stolen lives discloses the violence inherent in the structure of subjecthood that cops embody, protect, and are sanctioned to kill for. Sitting with these lives has required my attention. It has required my attentiveness.

ON NOT LOOKING AWAY: ATTENTIVENESS AS
THE SECOND STEP OF PARAPHENOMENOLOGY

Sitting-with requires that we don't move on, that we stay. In staying, we adopt a paraphenomenological stance; we sit with these lives as an enactment of philosophical criticism. But there is a bit more to sitting-with. If the first step is to not move on, then the second step is to not look away. Sitting-with requires that we focus on the lives, that we tend to them, that we attend to them. In other words, sitting-with requires that we become attentive. That's the second step.

I've shown a bit of this already, but I want to go further. Earlier, I mentioned that this text is an enactment of wake work. I therefore want to return to Christina Sharpe to show what I mean by sitting-with being a form of caring wake work that requires attentiveness.

From what I can tell, Sharpe isn't a phenomenologist, but she is certainly attentive. She's especially attentive to a photo of a young girl who was rescued from the 2010 Haitian earthquake. Across the girl's face is a piece of tape that simply says "SHIP." Sharpe sits with the photo. She stays with the girl. And the girl moves Sharpe; she is moved to ask questions, disruptive questions, about the meaning of that term: *ship*.[32]

> Is *Ship* a proper name? A destination? An imperative? A signifier of the im/possibility of Black life under the conditions of what, Stephanie Smallwood tells us, "would become an enduring project in the modern Western world [of] probing the limits up to which

it is possible to discipline the body without extinguishing the life within"? Is *Ship* a reminder and/or remainder of the Middle Passage, of the difference between life and death? Of those other Haitians in crisis sometimes called boat people? Or is *Ship* a reminder and/or remainder of the ongoing migrant and refugee crises unfolding in the Mediterranean Sea and the Indian and Atlantic Oceans?[33]

As the little girl looks back at the camera with that piece of tape on her forehead, she disrupts and discloses the manifold violence that comes with the meaning of *ship* and its disastrous legacies.

Notice that Sharpe doesn't make declarations; she asks questions. Notice how these questions come from her engagement with the young girl—which is to say, notice how Sharpe's attention is wholly invested in the young girl. Notice how this investment prompts a different line of engagement, one that doesn't overdetermine the meaning of the young girl in the photo, but instead draws Sharpe to take the young girl seriously. This young girl is real; Sharpe doesn't bracket her existence.[34] Sharpe doesn't reduce back from the girl. She stays with her; she allows her to guide her questions. The fact—not the assumption—of her existence prompts Sharpe to ask questions.

In fact, Sharpe's attention is so focused on this young girl that she returns to it. And in returning to it, Sharpe goes further than asking disruptive questions. She starts noticing things. She notices that "a life, however precarious, was always there. . . . I looked again at that photo and I marked her youth, the diagonal scar that cuts across the bridge of her nose and into her eyebrow, those extravagant eyelashes that curl back to the lid, the uncovered wounds, that bit of paper on her lip, and a leaf on the gown and in her hair. . . . *I had to take care*."[35] She notices the hints of life in that photo—eyelashes and a scar; a bit of paper and "a leaf on the gown and in her hair." And speaking of hair, she notices the little girl's braids. "And I think," she writes, "*Somebody braided her hair before that earthquake hit*."[36] Sitting with this photo, Sharpe notices life, black life, in the midst of the overwhelming and widespread "requirement for our death." Sharpe pays attention. No, that's not quite right: Sharpe has become attentive.

Becoming attentive means that we abandon the primacy of the first-person perspective. Notice that I say *the primacy* of the first-person perspective; we do not cease to exist when we sit with someone (if we did, we wouldn't be there to care for them). Sitting with this photo includes Sharpe, but it is not about her. She isn't the center of attention. Instead, Sharpe intensifies her attention. She focuses on the violence this young girl has suffered, as well as the care she's received. In sitting with the girl, Sharpe abandons her capacity, and perhaps her desire, to understand, because something else, something more important, is at stake: *I had to take care.*

This is what happens in this book. This book is a work in and of attentiveness. It describes encounters in sometimes painstaking detail. In describing these encounters, it notices hints of life within them—braids and hands (chapter 1), movement and speech (chapter 2), love and feeling (chapter 3). Noticing these things discloses how real these lives were and are, and it exposes what's at stake in the violence of these encounters.

TO THE LIVES THEMSELVES: PARAPHENOMENOLOGY
AS A CRITIQUE OF THE VIOLENCE OF ABSTRACTION

Sitting with these lives can undo us. It undoes our thinking—even if for a moment. In beholding these lives and deaths, we realize that they do not fully enflesh (the limitations of) the first-person perspective.

Something else occurs, too. Beholding these lives shows the violence of abstractions that come from the privileging of the first-person perspective. Abstractions are, after all, the result of looking away, of moving on, of not staying; they are what appear after reductions have been enacted. Consider it: notions like *black male* or *the suspect* are abstractions; they are categorical designations superimposed onto rich and complex black lives. And as I show throughout this book, such abstractions can and will kill; turning away can sanction and engender violence. The third step of sitting-with is to refrain from reducing lives to mere material for theory, for abstraction.[37]

Aiyana, Tamir, Alton, and Sandra remain opaque to us. Charles Long tells us that black lives "deny the authority of the white world to define their reality, and deny the *methodological* and *philosophical* meaning of transparency as a metaphor for a theory of knowledge," which means that black lives are not fully or easily captured by theoretical frames.[38] These lives exceed our frames of reference, our theories. They cannot be fully known. That is their beauty. That is their power.

According to Barbara Christian, theory fixes "a constellation of ideas for a time at least, a fixing which no doubt will be replaced in another month or so by somebody else's competing theory."[39] Making a theory out of these lives would produce a chain reaction in which we'd try to outdo each other in explaining these lives and deaths. It would then be about us. But perhaps more to the ethical point, making a theory out of these lives would situate them within a closed system, a set of definitions and logics that would foreclose their capacity to still speak—to keep speaking. Theory can't hold these lives.

But these lives do (prompt us to) theorize. "People of color have always theorized," Christian writes, "but in forms quite different from the Western form of abstract logic," and she "intentionally uses the verb form rather than the noun" because theorizing is dynamic; black lives still speak.[40] Even in and after their deaths, these lives remain opaque to us. They elude us. They escape our frames of reference. They are fugitive; and sitting with their fugitivity "sets in motion, or calls for, a form of supra-inhabitation of thought or demands that a certain meta-perspective take shape right in the midst of experience, self-consciousness, or the particularities of existence."[41]

Such a perspective would and does point us toward theoretical structures, but it does so in service of exposing, situating, and perhaps disrupting them in service of something more capacious, more ethical, more . . . engaged. As this book unfolds, you'll see what I mean. You'll see how Aiyana and Tamir were subjected to the violence of causal logics and theodicean structures (chapter 1); you'll hear how Sterling's movement and speech criticize certain philosophies of normative subject formation (chapter 2); and you'll witness how an affect like irritation can be deployed and manipulated to justify misogynoirist violence (chapter 3). Aiyana, Tamir, Alton, and Sandra are inscrutable lives that call us to see differently. And perhaps in seeing differently, we might be called to act differently.

Maybe that's the difference between phenomenology and paraphenomenology: it's the difference between turning to, and then turning away from, (knowable) objects on one hand, and turning to, and staying with, (inscrutable) lives on the other. Sitting-with, then, is a paraphenomenological—and therefore critical and constructive—method and disposition. Paraphenomenology is a criticism of phenomenology, but it is also a constructive act of care, of tending to black lives we've lost. If the phenomenological maxim is "to the things themselves," then perhaps the paraphenomenological maxim is "to the lives themselves."[42]

I guess, then, a definition is necessary: sitting-with is a radically critical disposition of care for, and attentiveness to, black lives; it is a paraphenomenological method of philosophical and religious criticism that exposes, criticizes, and disrupts dominant philosophical and religious modes of thinking and acting that sustain and reinforce antiblack violence. In sitting with these lives, you will see things differently. And, hopefully, seeing things differently might prompt you—us—to (continue to) act differently.

I therefore offer sitting-with as an encouragement and invitation: to (continue to) enact radical care.

Do you have a minute?

I do.

So does the movement for black lives.

Black *Lives* Matter: The Movement and Its Opening

In 2013, Alicia Garza, Patrisse Khan-Cullors, and Opal Tometti had a minute. In the wake of George Zimmerman's acquittal, Garza penned a Facebook post that told black people that we matter. Khan-Cullors and Tometti drew from Garza's passion, and a hashtag was born: #blacklivesmatter.

Their efforts were (unfortunately) quite timely: just a year after Garza wrote her post, Darren Wilson killed Michael Brown on August 9, 2014. In doing so, he set a (recent) precedent for shooting and killing black women, men, and children on camera and getting away with it. The people of Ferguson, Missouri, had had enough. And though they were not associated with the hashtag or the Black Lives Matter Network, they didn't need to be; the movement for black lives exceeded (and still exceeds) the network and the hashtag. The organizers in Ferguson had a minute, too, and they showed up in full force. The country was put on notice: black people were not going to take their deaths sitting down. The movement of black resistance in the United States was reincarnated. And, for better or worse, Khan-Cullors's name stuck: Black Lives Matter.[43]

The movement went national. Then it went international. People from England to Palestine were declaring Black Lives Matter. The movement spread, but it wasn't and isn't centralized. Each community organizes in ways that respond to the specific conditions in their specific locations. Perhaps, then, it is better to speak of the movement beyond the three words; what erupted in Ferguson is best understood as part of a larger movement (from and) for black lives.

The movement moves toward something that this world cannot understand; it expresses and organizes toward a vision of black life we cannot yet fully realize but we know is already here. Minkah Makalani writes that the movement "refuses [the] normative range of possibility and begins precisely with that which is impossible or nonsensical as thought and culls from the experiences of peoples and movements those worldviews, practices, and knowledges that enable us to move beyond the already available."[44] We see what cannot be seen. We yearn for what cannot be fully grasped. And we do so because we know it is possible, because we have felt it. Having sat with black lives in their own ways, thousands—perhaps millions—of people have been disruptive in service of something different, maybe even something better, something beyond what we are currently given. That disruptive movement is still going on. It hasn't stopped. And I doubt it will stop anytime soon.

Black *Life* Matter: Blackness as Living Matter

Obviously, with a title like *Black Life Matter*, I offer this book as a contribution to the movement for black lives; having organized, marched, and protested with people who were invested in black life, this book is a testament to those who have participated in a movement that began long before I existed and, sadly, will probably have to continue long after I'm gone.

This book, however, is not a chronicling of the movement. There are other powerful books and articles that handle the movement's unfolding far better than I could. Keeanga-Yamahtta Taylor and Barbara Ransby chronicled the movement's historical, political, and feminist contours and underpinnings; Christopher Lebron wrote an intellectual genealogy of the movement, distilling the philosophical underpinnings that motivate and sustain it; and Minkah Makalani and Debra Thompson have underscored the radical and affective power of the movement in articles.[45] I am indebted to these writers and others. They inform a lot of what I do here.

But this book has a different focus. Aiyana, Tamir, Alton, and Sandra call me to think about what it means when we say *Black Lives Matter*.[46] In thinking about this phrase, I couldn't help but hear the manifold notions of *matter* present in the phrase. On one hand, matter is that metaphysical substance that has been rendered mute in its presentation and mutable in its function. Placed in opposition to mind or spirit, matter has been configured as brute solidity, the res extensa of Cartesian thought that invites constraint and manipulation through its very extension—and therefore resistance—in the world. On the other hand, *matter* announces the possibility of mattering; to matter is to stand out, to exist, to emerge as that which is significant, even if such significance is rendered negative, violent, or even discardable. Matter matters.

Quiet as it's kept though, matter has always mattered. And, at least for some time, matter has been (figured as) black. In discussing the object—the form matter often takes in Western thought—Fred Moten makes this clear: "Blackness . . . is a strain that pressures the assumption of the equivalence of personhood and subjectivity. While subjectivity is defined by the subject's possession of itself and its objects, it is troubled by a dispossessive force objects exert such that the subject seems to be possessed—infused, deformed—by the object it possesses."[47]

Sitting with these lives makes explicit the very pressure of which Moten speaks, and this is precisely where I get my title from. Yes, *Black Life Matter* is a play on the phrase, but it is also meant to underscore how black lives move through the world as living matter or, put differently, how black lives move as flesh.[48] As I will show in a bit, flesh is not (yet) an object—or subject, for that matter.[49] It's an irreducible mode of life that grounds the subjectivity of the subject as well as the objectivity of the object. Black-life-matter is a mode of fleshy movement and engagement that sets the subject's violent thirst for clarity and transparent meanings in sharp relief.

Flesh is material; it leaves impressions, which means it can become objects. But it's sentient, too, which means that it lives.[50] Flesh is reversible; it feels and can be felt; it wounds and can be wounded; it gives and receives pleasure.[51] Flesh's reversibility calls the subject into question; it displaces the subject's primacy, (dis)possessing the subject in the process—and therefore compelling the subject to solidify the meaning of its existence. Flesh therefore grounds subjects through the violence they enact against it.

This is the case because flesh is irreducible to the significations superimposed upon it. Flesh "has no name"; it cannot be fully captured.[52] Turning flesh into objects therefore requires that it is reduced, flattened out, and made into something that can be grasped, apprehended, and understood; flesh becomes objects and subjects through "the calculated work of iron, whips, chains, knives, the canine patrol, the bullet."[53]

The black lives with whom this book sits show themselves as flesh. They exceed the ontological designations and constraints imposed upon them. They were made into objects—bodies (chapter 1), "a threat" (chapter 2), and a site of irritability (chapter 3)—through violence. But they also *lived*. Aiyana was sleeping; Tamir was playing when the cops came; Alton was speaking and moving throughout his encounter with the officers; Sandra showed irritation at the state trooper's ruse. And it was precisely this life that the officers could not stand.[54] In response, they enacted violence to clarify the primacy of their subjecthood.

BLACKNESS, FLESH, AND PLASTICIZATION

The subjects who encountered Aiyana, Tamir, Alton, and Sandra stretched their flesh out, pinned it down, warped and distorted it to make it do and mean what they wanted and needed. Zakiyyah Jackson calls this kind of violence "plasticization." "Plasticity is a mode of transmogrification whereby the fleshy being of blackness is experimented with as if it were infinitely malleable lexical and biological matter, such that blackness is produced as sub/super/human at once, a form where form shall not hold: potentially 'everything and nothing' at the register of ontology."[55] As "everything and nothing," flesh founds the normative world; the normative world, in turn, pays flesh back by plasticizing it, brutally stretching it out, and therefore rendering it available for manifold forms of manipulation and violence.[56] Plasticization makes living matter, black flesh, whatever it needs it to be.

I use the phrase *black flesh* intentionally. Plasticization exposes the inextricable connection between blackness and flesh: "The black(ened) are," Jackson writes, "defined as plastic; impressionable, stretchable, and misshapen."[57] Jackson also tells us that plasticization isn't arbitrary. She tells us that plasticization is "a form of *engineering*" that comes from the slave trade, and she highlights how "*slavery's technologies were not the denial of humanity but the plasticization of humanity*."[58] Enslaved Africans were framed—they were enframed—to be whatever the ruling class needed them to be; their flesh was framed to mean, do, and be what others wanted and needed. Blackness became "sub/super/human all at once."[59]

Slavery may no longer be legal (even as it still goes on), but blackness is still plasticized. Consider Michael Brown: Ferguson police officer Darren Wilson said that, when he encountered Brown, he encountered an "angry demon"—which is to say, he encountered the supernatural, the superhuman. But this label—*angry* demon—indicates that Wilson also saw Brown as irrational, as subhuman. And as it relates to the human part, consider that, in a deposition, Darren Wilson affirmed Brown's humanity.

QUESTION: You described Michael Brown as a demon or demon-like.

WILSON: Admitted.

QUESTION: A demon is not a human being.

WILSON: Admitted.

QUESTION: You did not view Michael Brown as a human being during this incident.

WILSON: Denied.[60]

Brown is, "all at once," sub/super/human. Which is to say, Brown is plasticized black flesh. And this serves to justify Wilson. Wilson absolves himself of any guilt by (en)framing Brown as superhumanly strong and subhumanly angry, yet just human in general. This is the technology of plasticization at work: plasticization (en)frames flesh—and therefore blackness—as absolutely available for the thoughts and desires of others, of subjects. Plasticity is the way black flesh, living matter, is (en)framed by subjects. The (en)framing is part of the game. The (en)framing *is* the game.

The Violence of the Subject

Subjects (en)frame. They plasticize black flesh. And they do this because, philosophically anyway, they are defined in and as their capacity to think, to reason, to make sense of themselves and the world.[61]

Black Life Matter has a very specific definition of thinking that will unfold throughout the chapters. For now, though, suffice it to say that thinking frames matter—it enframes matter—to know and understand it; thinking is an epistemological enterprise of instrumental reason. Thinking makes categories. It manufactures distinctions. It creates representations. It provides reason. It is bound by logic. Thinking is digital; it points. It points out—as in identifying, singling out, and apprehending. In short, thinking makes and reinforces rules; it maintains order, and it does so as an attempt to fully grasp the meaning of what it encounters.

But flesh is unruly; it arrives unannounced. Flesh is also disorderly; it doesn't submit to normal modes of thinking and understanding.[62] Because subjects are defined by their capacity to think, flesh—living matter, black-life-matter—poses a challenge to subjects. It exposes their fragility and dispossesses them of their primacy. For subjects, encountering flesh is akin to trying to read hieroglyphics.[63] They don't get it, but they want to. They need to; if subjects can't understand something, then their existence is threatened. They think in response, and therefore enact violence—the violence of abstraction made possible by the violent circularity of their first-person privilege. Subjects are defined by their capacity to think, but it is precisely this capacity that privileges *them*, makes *them* primary.

Thinking doesn't simply make subjects primary, though; it maintains their primacy—even after they've enacted violence. In the wake of their actions, subjects must ask themselves an ethical question: What have I done?[64] And this ethical question leads to an ontological one: Who or what am I to have done this?[65] These questions prompt subjects to reflect on the violence they've enacted. They think again. They think after. In reflecting on their violence, subjects report on their actions; they provide reason(s) for why they did what they did. And in so doing, they solidify themselves; subjects ontologically and ethically arrive as afterthoughts; they justify themselves through after-action reports.

Thinking, then, is not merely an epistemological enterprise. It has ethical and ontological implications. In sitting with Aiyana, Tamir, Alton, and Sandra, the violent ethical and ontological implications of subject formation are exposed. Throughout this text, we'll see that the officers who killed were compelled to do so; they were dispossessed by the black people, the black flesh, the living matter, they encountered. They were dispossessed of their primacy; they needed to regain control. So, they thought. They identified. They categorized and signified, constituting—carving—objects of their violence out of irreducibly indeterminate black flesh. These officers took lives as an act of reason. They did it to retain the norms of this world. They also thought in the aftermath of their violence; they provided justifications for what they did.

Ending these lives gave meaning to these officers' existence. Without fail, each of these officers (like so many others) framed their actions as part of their policing duties—which means they are (or were) cops *because* they killed, *because* they enacted homicide in the name of public safety.[66] Cops find meaning in the violence they enact; violence is what makes them who they are. It is the way they protect, serve, and enforce law and order. Thinking makes and restores order, and it does so by setting its sights on living matter.

There is no bright side here; sitting with these lives doesn't bring them back. But it does show a cruel irony: it exposes how thinking needs matter to secure its existence. I mentioned this earlier in my discussion of phenomenological intentionality; thinking needs something to think about.[67] This isn't limited to phenomenology; it pervades much of Western philosophy in general. Philosophers from Descartes to Kant to Hegel—and yes, even to Husserl—have claimed that thinking is impossible without matter. Thinking is not a self-starter. It might attempt—often successfully—to gain and maintain control, but it's parasitic; without matter, thinking has no place. It is rendered inert. It ceases to exist. In the end, matter *matters* to thinking.

If this is the case for thinking, then it's certainly the case for subjects. Subjects need flesh to secure their existence. They come into being through a "threshold of susceptibility and impressionability" that stretches far beyond their own capacities.[68] (According to Merleau-Ponty, they're made of it, but it doesn't appear that they see it this way.) If thinking is parasitic, then so are subjects; without flesh, they have no place. They are rendered inert. They cease to exist. In the end, living matter matters to subjects.

When I say that these four black lives matter, then, I'm not simply claiming that black lives already matter to black people and should matter to others; I am also, always, and already claiming that these black lives were and are the living matter that is central to how subjects understand themselves; I will show that these lives cannot help but matter to and for the thinking of this world. Black flesh, living matter, matters—epistemologically, ontologically, and ethically.

Religiously, too.

Religion: How (Living) Matter Comes to Matter

Throughout this introduction, I have mentioned that this book is an engagement with philosophy of religion, which is usually understood as a series of questions and logical puzzles that include (among other questions) proving God's existence, understanding the nature of religious experience, accurately describing the relationship between faith and reason, and solving (or at least responding to) the problem of evil. *Black Life Matter*, however, comes at philosophy of religion from another vantage point. It challenges philosophy of religion to sit with black lives in their unruly and disruptively fleshy presence. Sitting with these lives allows for a reckoning with philosophy of religion's problematic preoccupation with the same old questions and concerns—two of which are discussed at length throughout this book: religious experience and theodicy.

VIOLENCE AGAINST THE SACRED: SUBJECTS
AND RELIGIOUS EXPERIENCE

As living matter, flesh exceeds language: to engage with it, we need the imagination—which means, as Charles Long once observed, that we must engage religion and religious experience.[69] Or, as Rudolf Otto, a neo-Kantian philosopher of religion (and heavy influence on Charles Long) once put it, we must engage in the sacred.

Sacred is a tricky term.[70] I suspect the reason this is the case is because Otto used the term to describe a specific—and for many, empirically unverifiable—set of experiences. For Otto, experiencing the sacred is an affective, not necessarily rational, experience. It entails feeling fear and attraction at the same time. Think burning bushes here: Moses saw a burning bush and he was terrified and compelled—he couldn't leave, but he didn't want to stay, either. The sacred announces how faith exceeds—or is at least different from—reason. The contradictory nature of religious experience discloses the excessiveness of faith.

But we don't always believe in (allegedly) good things. The demonic, the monstrous—the threatening—are also part of faith traditions. As was stated earlier, Darren Wilson labeled Michael Brown as an angry demon; in chapter 2, we'll see a similar dynamic with Alton Sterling, and in chapter 3, we'll encounter a man who claims that he was concerned because Sandra Bland moved in a suspicious fashion.

Such descriptions feel threatening; they feel terrifying. Subjects encounter black flesh as fear inducing and therefore repulsive. But the attraction is there, too: chapters 2 and 3 also show that officers will shoot excessively; they'll linger, stay around, and not leave the scene—which is to say, they are compelled to stay and (over)react. Despite legal claims of cops being reasonable beings, officers will show that reason itself can show up as a compulsion—and therefore attraction—in the face of allegedly terrifying black flesh. In the wake of the violence they enact, cops claim that they had to do what they did, that the situation required nothing less than shooting, pinning, snatching, and brutalizing black life.

Sacredness does that to subjects, though. The sacred exceeds cognition: what appears doesn't conform to understanding. It doesn't make sense. And that's what subjects fear. Subjects need sense; they are defined by their capacity to make sense. In the face of unruly, excessive, and irreducibly indeterminate black flesh, subjects will become existentially afraid. They will fear for their lives, and they will compulsively fight back with all they have. They'll shoot indiscriminately and excessively. They'll make monsters out of lives. They'll claim that their actions were accidental. Subjects therefore use reason to make sense of the sacred. Reason is the way subjects retain their priority, their primacy, their privilege. Subjects do not abide the sacredness of blackness well, and, as I stated earlier, they are called to justify themselves in the wake of the violence they've enacted.

THEODICY: JUSTIFYING VIOLENCE AGAINST THE SACRED

Black Life Matter uses an old term in philosophy of religion to name this structure of justification: *theodicy*. Theodicy used to be about justifying God in the face of evil. But now, theodicy no longer needs God. It can simply be the process of identifying, categorizing, and ultimately eradicating what has been called evil. In this text—and especially in chapter 1—I show

how theodicy has become a modality of reason. It is a justifying logic that maintains the brutal normativity of the subject.

While I give theodicy explicit attention in the first chapter, a critique of its logic runs throughout this text. In chapter 2, an officer thanks his God for killing Sterling; in chapter 3, a state trooper justifies his actions by claiming that Sandra Bland's affective state put him in a state of heightened awareness and duress. These statements are theodicean in nature; they justify the goodness of the officers in the face of the allegedly terrifying or threatening (read: evil) presence of black flesh.

The officers enact theodicy in their recollections of events, but they are able to do so only because they act as enforcers of the norms of this world. In other words, the officers are called upon to eradicate what the world deems evil. The world, in turn, justifies their actions, their existence: juries hang themselves; indictments are few and far between; the twofold legal shield of *Graham v. Connor* and qualified immunity juridically protects officers; and legislatively, an allegedly divisive US Congress can agree across party lines that abolishing the police is a horrible idea. In short, the world sanctifies these outrageous and nightmarish enactments of violence by freshly minting them with the official governmental seal of approval. What all this means, then, is that this world mandates officers to kill black life in service of public safety—which is to say, as an act of eradicating evil.

This is how blackness, as living matter, comes to matter to the world of normative subjects: they encounter blackness, living matter, as terrifyingly sacred, and then they reduce—which is to say, kill or maim—it into objects that can be comprehended. This violence is then retrospectively justified through theodicean logics, and voila: another state-sanctioned theft of black life. All because officers of the state are ontologically, legally, politically, and culturally called upon to restore order to irreducibly indeterminate and sacred presence of black flesh.

But this isn't the whole story.

THE SACREDNESS OF BLACKNESS, OR THE MYSTICAL POSSIBILITIES OF BLACK FLESH

Aiyana, Tamir, Alton, and Sandra—among so many others—are, indeed, sacred to subjects. But, as flesh, Aiyana, Tamir, Alton, and Sandra also show the possibilities of black flesh, the possibilities that they incarnate beyond their deaths. Ashon Crawley calls this vibration: "Everything living and dead, everything animate and immobile, vibrates. Because everything vibrates, nothing escapes participating in choreographic encounters with the rest of the living world."[71] Flesh vibrates beyond the opposition of life and death. And because it does, these lives still speak. They can still be heard.

Perhaps it is this possibility of being heard that speaks to flesh's religious capacities, too. After all, "Blackness—through the flesh—would bear the trace of what in Western thought is called 'the religious,'" and it would do so "without being reducible to any one tradition."[72] Religious experience can and will entail violence, but it can also afford the opportunity for life. It can and will offer critical space for sitting with lives who exceed our logics, and who therefore terrify and awe subjects through their eruption and sustained existence. Religion can, and does, offer life and death—and often offers both simultaneously.

That *both* is what these lives show us.[73] They were subjected to violence against the sacredness of their existence—a violence that binds subjects to thought. And yet their sacredness speaks to a mode of life that exceeds the categorical, calculative, and signifying schemes that would seek to reduce them into merely corporeal bodies. Black experience is a living one, filled with dynamic relationality and sociality forged in the very crucible of death itself. Blackness lives beyond death; if, as Alexander Weheliye claims, "it's the end of the world," then blackness is that which has not only survived but also thrives in the collapse of the world itself.[74]

As living, sacred matter, black flesh announces the possibility of a modality of life beyond the subject. It will #SayHerName, announcing specificity, but it does so "in service of a collective function." Its agency is derived not from individual volition or desire but through its existence as flesh that demands to be loved. It "enacts Clearings" wherever it goes, speaking against and back to the world that would turn us into slop for hogs.[75] It conditions the subject—which means it matters to subjects. But it also announces its own inestimable significance, which means it matters to those who are excluded from the world of subjects. As living matter, blackness matters. It is black-life-matter.

This is what I mean by black-life-matter: it is the mode of existence that exposes, sustains, and calls this world and its subjects into question through its excessive, resistant, and care-filled presence in this world as flesh. Religious in structure, subjective in its unfolding, and black through its perpetual refusal of and resistance to the truth of the world through its existence as living matter, black-life-matter names the existential, ontological, ethical, and religious weight black lives carry. Black-life-matter names that black lives have significance, that—no matter what anyone says—they deserve radical and unyielding care.

Conclusion: On (Not) Moving On

Aiyana, Tamir, Alton, and Sandra are no longer physically with us. It is incredibly brutal and deeply painful that most of us have come to know of them only through their deaths. But while some have moved on, I haven't. I still mourn. I always mourn. I am in mourning. I am—which is to say, I exist as—mourning.

I also celebrate. I always celebrate. I am in celebration. I am—which is to say, I exist as—celebration. "That we have to celebrate is what hurts so much," Fred Moten writes: "Exhaustive celebration of and in and through our suffering, which is neither distant nor sutured, is black study."[76]

This text is black study; it is as much an elegy as it is a praise song. It struggles with the doubleness of black life and black death, to the point where I cannot help but conclude that in black life, we are in death, and in black death, we are in life. "I want . . . to declare that we are Black peoples in the wake with no state or nation to protect us, with no citizenship bound to be respected, and to position us in the modalities of *Black life lived in, as, under, despite Black death:* to think and be and act from there."[77] If all I did was sit with the violence, I would miss the fact that Aiyana, Tamir, Alton, and Sandra loved and were loved by others. I wouldn't notice that these lives moved and still move others, that they were and are still loved. The chapters are as generative as they are critical; they come from a contradictory space. They announce that our mourning is also celebration.

As I conclude, I want us to think about Eric Garner's and George Floyd's last refrain: "I can't breathe." Ashon Crawley tells us that *I can't breathe* "is not merely raw material for theorizing, for producing a theological and philosophical analysis." He continues:

> "I can't breathe" charges us to do something, to perform, to produce otherwise than what we have. We are charged to end, to produce abolition against, the episteme that produced for us current iterations of categorical designations of racial hierarchies, class stratifications, gender binaries, mind-body splits. "I can't breathe," Garner's disbelief, his black disbelief, in the configuration of the world that could so violently attack and assault him for, at the very worst, selling loosies on the street. "I can't breathe," also, the enactment of the force of black disbelief, a desire for otherwise air than what is and has been given, the enunciation, the breathing out the strange utterance of otherwise possibility.[78]

Crawley points us to how "I can't breathe" carries the violence of this world as well as the yearning and enactment of something else, something otherwise than—or, as I put it, something beyond—the violence of this world. This text therefore sits between mourning and celebration, between (Afro-)pessimism and (black) optimism. I stay in the tension because the lives and deaths call me to stay there.

I did not know Aiyana, Tamir, Alton, or Sandra personally. But I was a part of the movement. I marched for Sandra (her family calls her Sandy); I organized in her wake and therefore in her honor. And I wasn't alone. In chapter 3, I'll give a small bit of the story. But here, I want to say that these lives—as well as Trayvon Martin, Michael Brown, Eric Garner, Rekia Boyd, Korryn Gaines, John Crawford III, Walter Scott, Freddie Gray, Ahmaud Arbery, Tony McDade, George Floyd, Breonna Taylor, and so many others—have left an indelible mark on me.

In this text, I sit with four of them. But please know that, in researching this book, I have sat with others. It pains me that I couldn't sit with them in more detail here; their absence from this text is not any indication that they were less important. They have all left a mark on me; they have shifted the way I think, and they have prompted me to try to act differently. Which is to say, all those black lives *still* matter. They will *always* matter— to their families, to the movement, to me, and even to those who try to say otherwise.

I know this world has moved on. Subjects have attempted to drain these lives of their significance; we see names and faces appear on advertisements, on the front covers of magazines; we see their names headlining limp and vapid legislation. Having tried to use these lives up, this world and its normative subjects have moved on to the next problem.

But these lives aren't problems to be solved. These lives show us the violence of solving problems; they show us how thinking cannot sit with the plenitude of a life, how black-life-matter is an affront to the normative categories of an antiblack world. And yet, these lives also show us black-life-matter is a site of profound love and care. Aiyana, Tamir, Alton, and Sandy expose it all. Their lives matter—to me, to their communities, to their families and loved ones, and yes, to this world and its subjects. Their black lives matter.

I do not know why I'm repeating myself. Perhaps it is because I am constantly aware of what thinking does. Maybe it is because I worry that, for some readers, the lives will come secondary to them; I worry that some readers will try to find the theory, searching this book's pages for the theoretical parts that can be extrapolated from the lives themselves. In short, I worry that some readers will move on while reading. I cannot control for that, I know. But I do worry about it.

I guess I repeat myself, then, because I do not want to forget why I wrote this book. Crawley tells us that "I can't breathe" charges us to do something, "to perform, to produce otherwise than what we have." This book is my attempt to do that something. I do not know if this book will perform or produce otherwise, but I hope it does. After all, I wrote this book for those we've lost—and those lives are otherwise. Always. They still speak. They call to us. They call us to be attentive. They call us to stay. Which is to say, they call us to care.

This book takes care.

HANDS AND BRAIDS
BLACK BODIES AS MERE
CORPOREAL MATTER

What makes the police kill Black children, everywhere? Rifle through their clothing, write down their names, slap their faces, rough up their bodies, eat away their young days, breath in their breaths; wipe their hands on their little chests and along their legs, and clasp their wrists so tightly they atrophy. What a strange and ghoulish intimacy.—Dionne Brand, *The Blue Clerk*

Unthought Violence: Aiyana Stanley-Jones and Tamir Rice

Joseph Weekley wasn't thinking when he killed Aiyana Stanley-Jones.

> It's my gun who shot and killed a 7-year-old girl. . . . I pulled the trigger of that gun, unintentionally, and I didn't even know it at the time. . . . I knew it was my gun that went off because I was right there. Then I started freaking out a little bit.[1]

Weekley was the "lead commando" of Detroit's version of a SWAT team, called the Special Response Team (SRT). On May 16, 2010, around midnight,

Weekley and his SRT comrades served a warrant for someone who was supposedly living at Stanley-Jones's address.[2] As one of his teammates threw a flash-bang into the house, Weekley busted through the front door, turned right, and shot Aiyana once through the head, instantly killing her. He was eventually charged with involuntary manslaughter and went to trial. Twice. Neither trial produced a conviction. The court would not try him a third time.

In both trials, Weekley claimed the killing was accidental. He didn't intend to kill Aiyana, he testified. Although his finger was already on the trigger, he didn't feel himself pull it. The gun was the agent; it seemed to have shot on its own.

Well, that's not quite true: Weekley said the reason why the gun shot was because Mertilla Jones, Aiyana's grandmother, bumped him—well, she bumped the gun, causing *it*, not him, to shoot.[3] He couldn't remember pulling the trigger, but he did remember Mertilla. Especially her braids. "Her head was, kinda [Weekley stammers]—she had some sort of braids or something—'cause I remember seeing that, the braids, okay. Just the top of the head, she's kinda covered or draped, and she hits it down. As she hits it down, I start to pull [the gun] back. I hear the shot, and I immediately go."[4] Weekley's own actions are fuzzy to him, but Mertilla's "braids" are real. They were the culprit, sedimented within, and standing out from, other past actions he cannot recall. And you can't blame someone, let alone convict them, for something they don't remember doing. Or at least this is what part of the jury reasoned.

Blame is still necessary, though. Even if it is displaced. Someone or something must be responsible. Per Weekley's logic, if any*thing* was to blame, it was his gun—the trigger was too soft. And if any*one* was to blame, it was Mertilla—she bumped him. Along with Weekley's gun, Mertilla's braids help form the causal foundation of his thoughtless killing. Blame the braids— which is to say: blame Mertilla. Had she just controlled her body, Aiyana might still be alive.

Weekley doesn't mention the fact that his finger was already on the trigger. If it hadn't been, no bump, no matter how hard, would have prompted his fingers to shoot. "He was supposed to keep his finger off the trigger," Prosecutor Robert Moran said in his closing statement.[5] But he didn't. Weekley was already primed to kill. Serving an arrest warrant, and trained to use brute force, he'd already thought it through; he knew he might need to shoot at a moment's notice. There was no time to think. There was no need to think. Reflexes would have to do. Thoughtlessness was his defense, and Mertilla's body was his shield. The court obliged.

* * *

Fast forward four years. The day is November 22, 2014. While speaking with a priest at a church in Cleveland, Ohio, Timothy Loehmann and Frank Garmback received a call over their police radios. There was "'a male waiving [*sic*] a gun and pointing [it] at people' at the Cudell Recreation Center," the dispatcher said, describing the suspect as "a Black Male, camouflage hat, grey jacket, and black sleeves at or near the swing set."[6]

Loehmann and Garmback sped to the center and eventually found their "man." "As we were even with the swing set," Loehmann recalled, "we observed a male matching the description given by the radio."[7] As they got closer, Loehmann recalled, he began to engage the person, yelling "'show me your hands' as loud as I could." Garmback yelled the same thing. Nothing doing. The "suspect" wasn't responsive. With time running out, Loehmann reverted to his training. "I was trained to keep my eyes on his hands because 'hands may kill.' The male appeared to be over 18 years old and about 185 pounds."[8]

Loehmann stayed focused on those hands. This apparently large man kept moving them, ultimately putting them where they should never go. "The suspect lifted his shirt and reached down *into* his waistband. We continued to yell 'show me your hands.' I was focused on the suspect. Even when he was reaching into his waistband, I didn't fire. I still was yelling the command 'show me your hands.'"[9] Loehmann recalls that he "didn't fire," which allegedly meant that there was time to do something else. But the video doesn't show this. It all happens in two seconds. Loehmann's statement, then, glosses over the fact that he was reacting, that he was no longer deliberating about the situation. His training fully took over; he was just doing what he was taught. He'd become an automaton; his programming took over.

> We are taught to get behind the cruiser for cover. We are taught to shoot and move. You do not want to be a sitting target. . . . This was an active shooter situation.
>
> We are trained to get out of the cruiser because "the cruiser is a coffin." . . . With his hands pulling the gun out and his elbow coming up, I knew it was a gun and it was coming out. I saw the weapon in his hands coming out of his waistband and the threat to my partner and myself was real and active.

I fired two (2) shots. Based on "tap-tap," training, I shot towards the gun in his hand. After two shots, I went to the rear of the cruiser. . . . After suspect was down, I didn't know if the threat was over.[10]

The "suspect" *was* down, and he wouldn't get back up. He died later that day. In the face of a "real and active" threat, one must respond. Quickly. Reaction was the only option in an "active shooter" situation.

But not any old reaction; he'd been trained for this. *We are taught* and *we are trained* play over and over again in his statement, signaling the sedimentation of his training.[11] He already knew what to do. He didn't have to think because the thinking had already been done.

We now know that the "suspect" wasn't an adult, and the "gun" wasn't real. The "suspect" was twelve-year-old Tamir Rice, and the "gun" he had was an air pistol whose orange cap had fallen off, making it look realistic.[12] The dispatcher knew this: the 911 caller repeatedly suggested that the gun was "probably" a toy, and that the person holding the toy was probably a "juvenile," a child.[13] Let Loehmann tell it, though, he didn't know any of these details. He saw a man with a gun, and there was no time to do anything other than what he was trained to do. He reacted, and reaction and thought are not (necessarily) the same thing. Or so we're told.

Like Weekley, Loehmann's apparent thoughtlessness vindicated him. He didn't even make it to trial. Garmback didn't either. A grand jury dropped all the charges. In ways that are eerily similar to Weekley's trial, Loehmann's vindication hinged upon an external black body. Mertilla "bumped" Weekley, which is why he shot. And had Tamir not "appeared to be over 18 years old," and had his hands not "reached down *into* his waistband," things might have turned out differently. Or at least this is what Assistant District Attorney Timothy McGinty would have us believe. "It is likely that Tamir, whose size made him look much older and who had been warned his pellet gun might get him into trouble that day, either intended to hand it over to the officers or show them it wasn't a real gun. There was no way for the officers to know that, because they saw the events rapidly unfolding in front of them from a very different perspective."[14] With no pertinent knowledge, Loehmann allowed his training to do the thinking for him. All he saw were hands. All he needed to see were hands. And, upon seeing those hands, Loehmann stopped thinking.

* * *

Weekley and Loehmann tell different stories. They do, however, share one thing: they don't take responsibility for their actions. They weren't thinking when they killed, so they tell us; the deaths were either accidental or a necessary outcome of training.

And they weren't alone: many black lives have been sacrificed on the altar of the unthought. On March 21, 2012, Dante Servin indiscriminately shot into a crowd of black people, killing Rekia Boyd in the process.[15] Jeronimo Yanez claimed "he had no choice" when he gunned Philando Castile down in his car during a traffic stop.[16] And Mumia Abu-Jamal adds three more names to the still-growing list of unthought state-sanctioned violence:

> A young woman, engulfed in a diabetic coma while sitting in her car, is repeatedly shot by a corps of cops, who say they are threatened by her. Tyesha Miller, of Riverside, California becomes a statistic.
>
> A young man sitting in his car in North Philly is surrounded by a phalanx of armed cops whose guns are pointed at him from all points. He is ordered to raise his hands. When he does so, he is shot to death by one of the cops, who insists he saw a gun. Dontae Dawson becomes a statistic.
>
> An emigrant from the West African nation of Guinea comes to America, taking an apartment in New York's Bronx Borough. When four NYPD cops approach his door, reportedly because of a suspected rape (he was not a suspect), he is shot at 41 times. Nineteen shots hit him. Amadou Diallo was unarmed, and will never return to West Africa.[17]

Tyesha Miller, Dontae Dawson, and Amadou Diallo lost their lives to a lack of deliberation. Armed with guns, those officers shot—excessively, recklessly, thoughtlessly. "Stopping the threat" was the only thing on their minds—there was no time to think about whether or not the "threat" was a threat at all.

Lost to us in the very moments when deliberation was deemed no longer necessary, these lives form the foundation for their killers' innocence. Those deaths might have been tragic, but tragedy doesn't entail liability. Thoughtlessness makes no claims to responsibility. It affords no recourse to redress. It is its own mode of justification. These officers didn't think because they didn't need to think. The situations in which they found themselves were already prescripted; the black people who appeared before them were predetermined. Weekley's finger was already on the trigger; Loehmann shot within two seconds of his arrival. "Under an awful lot of pressure," the officers were "just doing their jobs."[18] And just doing your job doesn't require thinking. Or at least that's the story we're told.

These lives that were lost on the altar of thoughtlessness demand further investigation—and not simply from the journalist or the documentarian. Here, I sit with Aiyana and Tamir. Their lives, the rapid fashion in which they came to an end, and the correlative freedom of their killers, say something about what it means not to think, how thoughtless action enacted against black bodies can justify the alleged goodness, or at least innocence, of the subject.

Aiyana and Tamir's lives critique the history of philosophy, particularly the histories of phenomenology and philosophy of religion. By sitting with them, we catch a glimpse of thought's limitations. By sitting with them, we can distill thought's discomfort with plentiful and living (black) matter. We can see how black bodies justify thought through their appearance as unthought objects. And, in the end, we can see how black life matter becomes the material foundation for political and cultural theodicy.

Aiyana and Tamir teach us this. But they also show us that there is more. Inasmuch as Aiyana and Tamir expose thought's violence by exposing its limitations, they also show us that this isn't the whole story. They were more than what the officers said of and about them. They were more than hands; they were more than the tragic result of accidents. But that'll be discussed later. For now, we must sit with the thoughtlessness that conditioned Aiyana and Tamir's demise.

Un/thought Objects

Thoughtlessness has a history. According to Saidiya Hartman, when it comes to the United States, the history of thoughtlessness is intimately connected to the history of blackness. It comes to us through the figure of the slave: "On one hand," she says, "the slave is the foundation of the national order, and, on the other, the slave occupies the position of the unthought."[19] The slave, "unthought" as it is, forms the "national order."

The slave has been racialized at least since modernity. It coemerged with racial blackness. "There was [and is] no relation to blackness outside of the terms of this use of, entitlement to, and occupation of the captive body," Hartman writes, "for even the status of free blacks was [and is] shaped and compromised by the existence of slavery."[20] The slave racializes blackness. The slave holds blackness hostage, not simply to the whims of the captor, but also to the body blackness has been forced to occupy. A syllogism emerges: the slave is the captive body; this captive body gets coded as black; and blackness, no longer able to fashion a name for itself, is ensnared in the process. Blackness—and in this case, black bodies—can therefore appear as that which is unthought, as that no longer in need of deliberation.

Hartman describes the relationship between blackness and the body as a "corporeal malediction," a near-unbreakable curse that reduces blackness to "the purportedly intractable and obdurate materiality of physiological difference."[21] Blackness becomes reduced to mere corporeality; the person who sees blackness only sees a black body. *The male appeared to be over 18 years old and about 185 pounds. . . . This was an active shooter situation.*

Once blackness becomes merely corporeal black bodies, it becomes an object. It is subjected to thought, to the whims of the subject. Corporeally maledicted, the black body is "a body that you can do what you want with."[22] It is bound to and by the consciousness of another. It is enslaved "to [its] appearance." Black bodies show up as phenomenal content beholden to an external gaze that sets upon it. They are held captive to perception, to recollection, to experience. They are the result of intentional experiences. *I remember seeing that, the braids.*

Michel Henry highlights that "intentionality . . . takes on the function of rationality." Intentionality names reason. It is the phenomenological—which is to say, the experiential—term for thought.[23] Sara Ahmed elaborates by claiming that thought begins in orientation, structured by one's relation to the entity, matter at hand, or task at hand that occupies subjective engagement.[24] We're already thinking the moment we direct our attention toward something.

But the relationship between thoughtful intentionality and thoughtless reaction is a close one. They invoke one another. Seeing something means you're not seeing (or at least not paying attention to) so many other things that are happening. Those other things are part of a horizon that makes seeing possible.

This horizon, however, is rarely thought, let alone thought about. Ahmed makes this clear: despite Edmund Husserl's careful thinking about the tables and paper upon which he writes, there is already a more expansive context that makes such thinking and writing possible: kids playing outside, Husserl's wife's unacknowledged labor.[25] This unthought horizon informs, frames, and conditions intentionality. Thought pays attention, but it can only pay attention to so much. To think is to be already steeped in unthought matter.

Matter is still there, though. It hits; it leaves a mark. Matter makes impressions. These impressions are hyletic; they might become tables, chairs, and bodies, but that comes after. Impressions are nonintentional, undirected.

"Material content," Michel Henry writes, "carries an essential trait within itself: it is the non-intentional and at the same time . . . the impressional and the affective." Intentionality—thought—gets going because it encounters excessive matter that makes an impression.

But material excess doesn't go unpunished. It's too much. It exposes thought's limits. It forces thought to reckon with its own negation. So, "just doing its job," intentionality, thought, fashions objects out of matter. It makes things out of impressions.

Material impressions are sensory.[26] We touch, taste, smell, and hear them. They are part of sensation. And sensation, like the matter that catalyzes it, exists prior to and beyond the emergence of the object. Sensations, like matter, are too much; what is sensed exceeds one's ability to understand its meaning. But this won't do. Sensation cannot be left alone. Contact induces the subjective compulsion to think and therefore name: a stubbed toe becomes a bedpost; a bump becomes braids. In the process, what was too much has now become just enough. The object is born. What is sensed makes possible what is signified.

But thought doesn't do this on its own absolute authority. There are rules. And thinking, if it isn't about anything else, is about rules.[27] Thought makes objects by forcing matter to obey rules it didn't make and for which it cannot control.[28] Will, volition, and desire are no longer possible. Once matter becomes objects, it no longer has a say. Making an impression on the subject, matter encounters and endures an objectifying violence not of its own making. The object is the effect of cognitive power exacted against irreducible and unthinkable materiality.

Thought distills plentiful material sensations into objects that can be— and already are—apprehended and comprehended. Hyle becomes captive to cognition through this very reduction; intentionality seizes sensation, descending upon it and holding it hostage to the consciousness that intends it. An object therefore appears, signified, available, ready for use; it has no say in its availability. It does not know the name it was given, but it is forced to respond to it. Already signified, the object is a construction, an invention, fashioned out of unthinkable matter making unthought impressions.

The object is, therefore, nothing less than the appearance of an entity already captive, already held hostage to the consciousness that subjects it to its whims. The object is not simply the symbol of captivity. It is its very appearance.

One would be mistaken not to see the correlation between captive objects and black bodies.[29] Hartman named this correlation a corporeal malediction; Frantz Fanon famously and rightly claimed that he was an "object among other objects."[30] And Judith Butler tells us that "what constitutes the fixity of the body, its contours, its movements, will be fully material, but materiality will be rethought as the effect of power."[31] Black bodies are objects, and these objects instantiate, express, and (unfortunately) maintain the status of normative power relations. Loehmann shot because he saw a large, black, male body—which is to say, he saw an object. Tamir had no say in the process. Aiyana Stanley-Jones died because Weekley was bumped by an object; even in speaking, Mertilla had no say in the matter.

Some would claim otherwise. Merleau-Ponty, for example, took the body as a starting point for thinking about freedom, agency, desire, and the like. He, like his teachers, understood the body as a living body. But even phenomenologists know better than to think that the living body is the only body. Husserl noted that there is a distinction between the "physical body [*korper*]"—what Fanon called "an object among other objects"—and the "lived body [*leib*]" upon which much of phenomenological theorizations about consciousness, movement, freedom, agency, intersubjectivity, and desire are founded.[32]

Husserl's *korper*, bound to and by intentionality, is therefore a spatio-temporal object determined by consciousness. It need not live—at least not in the phenomenological sense. *Korper* has no constitutive capacities; it cannot make or even siphon meaning; it does not wield the power to signify—it is only signified. Mere corporeality is already the space of objectified matter; hyletic and sensory impressions are its only mode of speech. *Korper*, the objective body, is always and already stripped of its will and desire. *It is likely that Tamir, whose size made him look much older . . . either intended to hand it over to the officers or show them it wasn't a real gun. There was no way for the officers to know that, because they saw the events rapidly unfolding in front of them from a very different perspective.*

Seeing, Smelling, and Touching Black Bodies

As an object, Husserl's *korper* comes to us through sensory impressions. This is precisely what happens with corporeal malediction: upon being cursed to the merely corporeal, blackness comes to us through the senses.[33] If the black body stands in for "obdurate and intractable physiological difference," it is because this difference is felt. It is seen, heard, smelled, touched, and sometimes tasted. Once blackness is corporeally maledicted, it becomes black *korper*.

Black *korper* is seen. Sight governs the perception of blackness-turned-black-bodies. After all, sight is philosophy's primary sense.[34] Already tasked with apprehending a "black Male," Loehmann eyeballed Rice's age and weight, concluding at a glance that "the male appeared to be over 18 years old and about 185 pounds."[35] Tamir was dead moments later. Sight can kill.

Tamir's appearance cannot be overstated. A group of social psychologists invited 116 police officers to participate in a study where their implicit and explicit associations of race with age, criminality, and use of force in children of various races were measured.[36] The results are disturbing, even if they may not be surprising: officers consistently overestimated the age and culpability of black children in ways that dehumanized them beyond the point of innocence: "The present research suggests that black children may be viewed as adults as soon as 13. . . . In other words, our findings suggest that, although most children are allowed to be innocent until adulthood, Black children may be perceived as innocent only until deemed suspicious."[37]

The authors conclude on a damning note. "These findings demonstrate that dehumanization of Blacks not only predicts the racially disparate perceptions of Black boys but also predicts racially disparate police violence toward Black children in real-world settings."[38] When viewed in light of McGinty and Loehmann's comments, this study makes clear that Rice was killed because he was seen—and then perceived—as a threatening, fully adult man who needed to be stopped, and this perception had everything to do with Rice's black body. *We observed a male matching the description given by the radio.*

Seeing black bodies takes practice. It has become a praxis. And it began long before Loehmann saw Tamir and Weekley encountered Mertilla. As Andrew Curran tells us, seventeenth-century intellectuals attempted to find the source of black skin. Marcello Malpighi, for example, blistered the skin of a black man and found a layer of pigmentation that, he concluded, was the source of blackness in black bodies.[39] This layer would be subsequently named the Malpighian layer, wherein most of the melanin in one's skin is produced and contained.[40]

The investigations went beyond skin. But they were almost always governed by sight: "darkened bile" stained blood and skin; black brains were literally darker than white ones; and even black men's sperm was black.[41] Seeing blackness everywhere, these intellectuals perceived black bodies as objects of scientific and anatomical analysis. They made a practice out of seeing, blistering, dissecting, and then comprehending black bodies. Sight governed the science of racial anatomy. And this sight engendered violent insights—which, in turn, engendered physical violence. Tamir was killed on sight; doesn't that matter?

Sensory reception isn't simply reducible to sight. Blackness was, and still is, perceived through other senses. In *How Race Is Made*, historian Mark Smith makes a compelling historical case that all the senses were used to detect and signify blackness. Black bodies were heard as loud and cacophonous; they were tactilely felt as having stronger, more obdurate skin; and, perhaps only second to sight, olfaction—smell—was principally determinant in discerning the presence of blackness.[42] Smith begins his text with an interesting anecdote: while he was at an all-white dinner party one day, one of the guests felt free to share the following story.

> "My grandmother . . . years ago, probably in the [nineteen] twenties . . . left her house on some errands. She returned, walked in, and discovered her house had been broken into." He paused.
>
> "Know what she said?" He knew how to tell a story—as I said, a southerner. I shook my head.
>
> "I smell nigger."[43]

Smell became an investigatory tool, harnessing the powers of the nose to determine the racial identity, and therefore culpability and criminality, of an unknown suspect. The grandmother smelled "nigger"—which is to say, she smelled guilt.

People still smell nigger. Journalist Sara Koenig recalls how olfaction was used in both determining and solidifying black criminality through the sense of smell. A young man named Aramis Spencer was attempting to get a cigarette from one of his neighbors in an apartment complex. Two officers saw him, searched him, and found marijuana on him. They attempted to arrest him, but he asked why, and things escalated from there, as the officers proceeded to beat and eventually arrest him on charges of drug possession, suspicion of robbery, and resisting arrest.[44]

When the case went to trial, one of the officers made an interesting claim: "I walked past him. And as I approached him, I smelled the odor of marijuana. It got stronger—it was clearly coming from him."[45] As crucial as this claim is for justifying why the officers beat and eventually arrested Spencer, it is nevertheless specious. Sara Koenig claims that "marijuana [was] not scarce" in the building where Spencer lived.[46] But somehow, the officer claimed to smell it emanating specifically from Spencer himself, and it was precisely this smelling that lent itself to solidifying Spencer's criminal culpability. There was already an impressional context—smelling weed—that governed the officer's perception. Aramis Spencer was criminally charged as a result.

Subjects touch black bodies, too. Smith records the history of black touch through perceptions of black skin as more durable than other skin. But Mertilla Jones offers another trajectory of tactile blackness: the bump. According to Weekley, Mertilla allegedly "bumped" him "in a downward motion," occasioning Weekley to pull the trigger. In so doing, Weekley wove a sensory web of tactility and sight to disclose the actual source of his infanticidal "accident." Sight and touch collapsed into one another; the bump could not be disentangled from the braids. Weekley killed Aiyana because he sensed—he saw, he touched—blackness.

Black *korper* is sensed. The above is only a sampling; black bodies are heard and tasted, too. But no matter the sensory capacity, sensation and signification work with one another; sensing *makes sense*. In the presence of the black body, the term *sense* carries its original double meaning. There is already a historical association of guilt, a negative valuation, a threatening appellation—a *malediction*—tethered to the sensory reception of black bodies. Corporeal maledictions may come from phenomenological reductions to mere corporeality, but they are still evil words.[47]

Signifying Black Bodies: Black Bodies as Un/thought and Un/gendered Equipment

Making these malevolent associations used to take practice. The "attenuated meanings, made an excess in time, over time, assigned by a particular order," are now second nature for black bodies.[48] Loehmann's actions, Aramis Spencer's case, and the psychological study all speak to the unthought associations that occur because of blackness's corporeal presence. These officers—both in the study and in the field—sensed blackness as black bodies, with all the attendant meanings that come with them. When it comes to black bodies, sensing signifies.

Signifying is a power.[49] It is the ability to classify, categorize, and conceptualize. It is the power to objectify. Historian of religions Charles Long tells us that signifying bypasses "the active existential and self-identifying *notae* through which a people know themselves."[50] The signifier need not listen to what it signifies.

Long first published those words in 1986. Just a year later, Hortense Spillers also wrote about signification. But she talked about names. "Let's face it. I am a marked woman, but not everybody knows my name. 'Peaches' and

'Brown Sugar,' 'Sapphire' and 'Earth Mother,' 'Aunty,' 'Granny,' God's 'Holy Fool,' a 'Miss Ebony First,' or 'Black Woman at the Podium': I describe a locus of confounded identities, a meeting ground of investments and privations in the national treasury of rhetorical wealth. My country needs me, and if I were not here, I would have to be invented."[51] These externally imposed loctions wrap Spillers (and the women she stands in for) in a semiotic straitjacket; they "isolate *overdetermined* nominative properties. . . . They demonstrate a sort of telegraphic coding; they are markers so loaded with mythical prepossession that there is no easy way for the agents buried beneath them to come clean."[52] Buried beneath signs they did not give themselves, black people struggle to get out from under the webs of meanings that are black bodies.

I didn't slip the black body in just now. Spillers herself makes a correlation between signifying and black bodies, for they are "disrupted . . . by externally imposed meanings and uses," one of which is "*being for* the captor."[53] Black bodies are already captured; they are the property of others who have the power to name them without their consent.

Having become property, black bodies are available for use. They become equipment.[54] And equipment is necessary. One uses equipment in service of finishing a project. And imagining, working toward, and completing projects secures one's subjectivity.[55] Utility invokes necessity; use requires something *of* use. *My country needs me, and if I were not here, I would have to be invented.*

Need doesn't necessarily entail visibility, however. Tools recede from view in the act of use. They become unthought. As Martin Heidegger makes clear, one does not think about the hammer in the act of hammering; one hammers. Though it was constructed as a tool, using the hammer obscures the history of its invention. Even though they were invented long ago, hammers no longer need deliberation, especially when they're being used. When one hammers, the hammer becomes part of the subject. The subject takes primacy; all that remains is the task at hand and the subject who is completing the task. In the act of hammering, the hammer is unthought.

The introductory clause to the last sentence is crucial; people still think about hammers. They just don't think about them while using them. If they do, it's because something has stopped the workflow. Heidegger tells us that tools become visible when they fail to do or be what they are supposed to. One doesn't think about what a hammer is until it goes missing or it breaks.[56] If it's lost, one tries to find it. If it's broken, one examines it, trying to find where the break occurred. And if one cannot fix or find the tool, one will simply replace it. The tool becomes fungible; any hammer will do.[57] Thinking about tools returns them to their proper roles, and once that order has been restored, once one fixes or replaces the tool, one goes back to no longer thinking about it. Instrumental reason thinks so that it might think no longer.

Black bodies are tools. They are equipment. They invoke schemas of function and dysfunction, of thoughtless engagement and thoughtful deliberation; they are subjected to utilitarian schemas of existential and ontological importance. Regarding Aiyana and Tamir, there may be no clearer evidence for this utilitarian schema than what happened to Mertilla Jones and Samaria Rice, Tamir's mother. (You don't invoke "Mama's Baby" without thinking about gender—and its undoing.) Because they are circumscribed by their utility and invented out of necessity, black bodies—particularly black female bodies—disintegrate a (more or less) stable and coherent gendered matrix.[58] Gendering hammers makes no difference in their subjection to the whims of the subject.[59]

This is precisely what happened to Mertilla Jones. Recall that Weekley stated, "It was my *gun* who shot and killed a 7-year-old girl." Weekley personalized his gun, and therefore started the logical line of thinking that absolved him of agential—and therefore ethical—responsibility. But had he stopped at his gun, he'd have no case. He was charged with involuntary manslaughter and reckless discharge of a firearm; the gun was part of the charge. The gun, therefore, couldn't stand alone—jail time would be on the other side. So, he remembered (or conjured?) Mertilla's "braids."

(Brief aside: I put "braids" in quotes because I'm not actually sure Mertilla was wearing braids. It is possible that Weekley didn't simply conjure Mertilla as hair, but also conjured her particular hairstyle. Black hair, and particularly black women's hair, is irreducible to just braids. But "braids" serve an identifying function, as they rhetorically and metonymically act as a stand-in for black hair—and black women's hair more specifically. Weekley invoked "braids" as part of a utilitarian schema of identification; by conjuring "braids," he was conjuring Mertilla in her specificity as the black body that bumped him—and therefore as the real culprit of the violence. "Braids" were Weekley's tool of vindication; he used them to displace the responsibility of Aiyana's death from him onto her grandmother.)

In remembering (or conjuring?) Mertilla's "braids," Weekley necessarily remembered (or conjured) Mertilla. In fact, Mertilla came first. On the same day Weekley killed Aiyana, the *Bay View* reports, "Assistant Chief of Police Ralph Godbee claimed at a press conference . . . that Mertilla Jones had confronted or 'had contact' with the officer who shot Aiyana, causing his gun to go off accidentally."[60] Without the gun, Weekley doesn't shoot; but without the "braids"—which is to say, without Mertilla—the killing couldn't be accidental.

You'd think that braids would signal something like gender. After all, braids are often coded as female, especially when it comes to black women. There were other markers of gender (or at least normative gender), too: Mertilla's emotions and grandmaternity were on full display during trial. On the stand, Jones emotionally protested against Weekley's story. She tearfully claimed, "You know I never touched you, Mr. Weekley." Jones also testified that, immediately after Weekley killed Aiyana, she told the SRT, "Y'all killed my grandbaby."[61] With tears in her eyes on the stand, Mertilla Jones established herself as Aiyana's grandmother. She named and made explicit her matrilineal role in Aiyana's life.

But none of this mattered. In fact, the judge censured Mertilla before she took the stand again. "We all know that you're hurting," the judge said. "It doesn't call for us not respecting each other."[62] Mertilla's emotions offered nothing; though she was Aiyana's grandmother, and though she, too, was present at the scene, her testimony went unheeded.

In fact, Mertilla's own words could and would be used against her. Reporter Gus Burns suggested that Mertilla's testimony could in fact be what helped to vindicate Weekley: "It is her changing story and other inconsistencies that could seal a not-guilty verdict for Weekley," Burns writes. The "changing story" to which Burns refers is the fact that "soon after the death, Jones said she believed the gunshot came from outside," whereas "in a court . . . she described the shooting more like an assassination."[63]

Burns, however, fails to mention that Jones was consistent in claiming that she never touched Weekley. She repeatedly testified that Weekley pulled the trigger on his own. But such a claim doesn't even show up in Burns's reporting. Jones's testimony was less important than her body; her presence at the scene outweighed the veracity of her speech. During the shooting and at trial, Jones was nothing more than a body "[severed] from its motive will, its active desire."[64] Having had the most significant dimensions of her testimony unheard, Jones's desire to speak and therefore to be heard fell away. Her intentions, her desires, were not important.

Even her relation to Aiyana wasn't important. Despite being at the scene, and despite being Aiyana's grandmother, Mertilla's testimony wasn't taken seriously enough. Maternal relation couldn't stop Weekley's vindication. Even grandmotherhood couldn't stem the ungendering effects of corporeal maledictions.[65] Whether understood as trope or disposition, the "mother" ceases to carry with it the kind of normative gendered weight that it might have if the "woman" in question were white. Destabilizing gender's normative matrix through what could be understood as a gendered concept, the black mother does not stop the violence enacted against black female flesh in the name of already signified and merely corporeal black bodies. Grandmother or not, Mertilla's body was present. That's all that mattered.

Mertilla isn't alone. Samaria Rice, Tamir's mother, also fell prey to the ungendering dynamic that is black motherhood. Even though Rice may have been the specific body upon which Loehmann's training was enacted, Samaria Rice somehow was also to blame. After Loehmann killed Rice, articles surfaced about Samaria's criminal record, claiming that Samaria "set a bad example" for Tamir, making the implicit suggestion that her motherhood was somehow insufficient.[66] Even school officials got in (on) this. As Sheryl Estrada reports, a school resource official called Samaria a stupid "b**ch" for "allowing" her son to be killed.[67]

There are other moments when Samaria's parenting was taken seriously—but only to blame Tamir. As I showed above, DA McGinty stated that Tamir "had been warned that his pellet gun might get him into trouble that day"; this warning rhetorically acts as protection against Loehmann's recklessness, invoking Samaria's maternal injunctions only to lay culpability at her son's feet in the process. Samaria's words and actions were already overdetermined by a sociolegal context of black criminality and maternal failure. Samaria's words and actions may have stemmed from her body, but they were not, or at least no longer, her own. Whatever "active desires" Samaria had for her son were mutated into evidence for Tamir's lack of judgment. (Never mind that he was thirteen years old.)

Kimberly Juanita Brown writes that "motherhood is a problematic aspect of black diasporic relations," and the invocation, denigration, and sublimation of Samaria's parental injunctions and capacities sets this problematic aspect in full relief.[68] Either Samaria wasn't a good mother, or her mothering was ineffective—which is to say, she wasn't a good mother. Either way—which is the same way—Samaria's motherhood became a rhetorical, political, legal, and ontological tool deployed in service of ensuring that Loehmann was not to blame.

Brown asks, "What are the possibilities for self-possession in the context of black maternal investment?"[69] In Samaria's case, such possibilities are limited at best and nonexistent at worst; her words were not hers; her injunctions were not hers. One might even say that Samaria's body wasn't hers, as it was conjured to solidify the innocence of others. Her gender was invoked only after—but for very specific reasons; her motherhood emerged only after people realized that Loehmann had, indeed, killed a child. Motherhood showed up, but it was disfigured. Gender was invoked, but not for Samaria's benefit—only to her discredit.

Spillers tells us "it would appear reactionary, if not dumb, to insist on the integrity of female/male gender," and this could not be truer for black female bodies.[70] In fact, given the black body's existence as "being for" captors, one might suggest that gender's disruption and its sustenance come through the utilitarian schema attached to black bodies. Aiyana and Tamir's killers are free; neither Mertilla nor Samaria could escape the culpability assigned to them, even as they occupied grand/maternal roles in the lives of these children. In a riff off Judith Butler, we might say that black bodies are the matter out of which gender is fashioned—even if, or maybe even because, such fashioning is not extended to include them.[71]

It didn't matter that Mertilla is a woman; all that mattered, and all that still matters, is that she was a body that became the primary cause of accidental homicide. The braids were only an identifying marker; they named Mertilla as the body present at the scene. Her words meant (little to) nothing—Mertilla Jones was not Carolyn Bryant. And Samaria's mothering was nothing less than a site for the exploitation of others; her motherhood was mined for its ability to reproduce various defenses for Loehmann. Samaria and Mertilla's gender, should it be so named, offered no alternatives.

But make no mistake: Mertilla and Samaria were still needed. They were necessary. Though they were reprimanded, denigrated, and siphoned for their grand/maternal relations to Weekley's and Loehmann's victims, they were nevertheless made to be always and already available for exploitation against their will. They were conjured as instruments, buried beneath the necessary significations that enabled other existential projects. Mertilla and Samaria are not hammers. But the world certainly treated them like they were.

Of Black Bodies and Bridges: Black Bodies as Material Sites of Theodicean Justification

The history of the corporeally maledicted black body invokes various schemas—material, sensory, signifying, and utilitarian. Black bodies are the unthought result of thinking's encounter with unthinkable black life matter. Matter makes an impression through sensing; sensing attends to and is attended by signification; signification objectifies; and objects are instrumentalized. Don't read the earlier sentence in a linear fashion. Like the late Heidegger's bridge, black bodies gather materiality, sensation, signification, and utility through their presence. To think with one dimension of the corporeally maledicted black body, to think with black *korper*, is to already think of the other three.

Like Heidegger's bridge, corporeally maledicted black bodies are not some fifth thing operative outside of the schemas they gather; instead, they are ontic sites wherein ontological deliberation can, will, and does occur. And central to ontological deliberation is dwelling. Subjects cannot help but dwell—Heidegger lectures that dwelling is what constitutes the subject's being—which means that subjects cannot help but use bridges. Bridges are therefore invented as entities through which home is secured; the bridge makes subjective engagement possible.

In gathering and supporting the fourfold, bridges justify the fourfold's existence. The gods find a place to gather; mortals drive and walk upon the bridge; earth and sky make their appearance in and through its use. All of this goes unquestioned, and it is precisely this unquestioned and un-questionable dynamic that is violent and prompts more violence. After all, bridges have no say in whether they want to gather the fourfold; the four-fold dwells as its own justification. The one who dwells is the one who *can* dwell; the one who can dwell is the one who *should* dwell. Dwelling justifies the goodness of the fourfold—which is to say, dwelling is a theodicy.

As many black and womanist theologians have discussed, black bodies are religious and theological objects; from lynching to mass incarceration, black bodies are sites of justification and vindication.[72] Having become sensory sites of criminality, they are tools of rationalization and world building; having become spatiotemporal objects out of place, they emerge as material vestiges of theodicean reasoning. Black *korper* is conjured (up) to reinforce the normativity and order of the world.[73]

Such was certainly the case for Aiyana and Tamir: Weekley and Loeh-mann weren't convicted—Loehmann wasn't even charged. Weekley and Loehmann made their home, secured their dwelling, through the violent killing and denigrating use of black bodies. They justified themselves through homicidal violence. Juxtaposed with (or against) their victims, they became agents of justice and public safety.

These officers aren't one-offs. Though the data remains murky, multiple sources have confirmed that most officers aren't even prosecuted, let alone convicted, of lethal violence. Janell Ross reports that between 2005 and 2019, "98 nonfederal law enforcement officers have been arrested in connection with fatal, on-duty shootings," and only thirty-five of those arrested have been convicted.[74] While Derek Chauvin was tried and convicted for his heinous actions, the structure of justifying police violence remains intact.

There is more. Multiple sources confirm that black people are more likely to be killed by cops than their white counterparts.[75] Like so many other officers, Loehmann and Weekley enacted homicidal violence in the name of comfort. They killed so that the public might dwell, and dwell comfortably. Black *korper* secures the dwelling of others. A waistband is a threat; accidents are forgiven when braids enter the scene. Black *korper* are, indeed, bridges. The subject justifies its goodness by using them—even if use entails killing.

Utilitarian justification is a mode of thoughtlessness. Weekley's finger was already on the trigger—all he needed was something to prompt him to shoot. Loehmann was already prompted to shoot—his training told him what to do. Weekley and Loehmann thought about their actions after, but only to retain their existence as dwelling subjects in the world. No longer thinkable, merely corporeal black bodies occasion the possibility of subjective reflection and subjective justification.

Thoughtlessly Oriented Subjects: Black Bodies, Religion, and Subjectivity

Hartman was precise and accurate in her word choice: corporeal maledictions are, indeed, curses. They are forms of sociopolitical conjuring that warps perception. And these curses invite meditation on questions of religion and subjectivity. The question is not whether black people are, or could be, subjects; black bodies foreclose that question. Volition, agency, and freedom are perpetually deferred realities in black life, such that whatever subjectivity black people might express is always forced to wrestle with the "mythical prepossession" that entails an overdetermined existence. Conjured as utilitarian and theodicean bridges that justify the subject's normativity, black bodies disclose the relationship between religion and subject formation in the maintenance of this world.

The subject is one who can rest in the benefits it accrues from accursed black bodies. The subject is the one who can legitimately wield the power of corporeal malediction; it is the one who, in the presence of black bodies, need not think. Rest is central here. Rest signifies dwelling, and such dwelling is possible only if one is already at home in the world, already oriented toward the world as a space of familiarity and comfort.

Charles Long tells us that religion is "orientation in the ultimate sense."[76] Religion orients the subject. It gives the subject an opportunity to make sense of itself in relation to its surroundings. Sara Ahmed claims that "the question of orientation, becomes . . . a question not only about how we 'find our way' but how we come to 'feel at home.'"[77] Orientation is also about home, about how one comes to be at home in the world. It is the subject's way of making a home in the world, and of making sense of who and what can be at home in the world. In other words, orientation requires making distinctions. Orientation is possible only in relation to objects and others, and to othered objects: "The familiar is shaped by actions that reach out toward objects that are already within reach."[78]

Ahmed goes on to discuss "reach" as an embodied modality of orientation, but what I want to emphasize is the "already within reach." Already present, already there and "ready-to-hand," the objects that are within reach are already given, already offered up as perpetually available for use. Objects—whether they are bridges, hammers, or merely corporeal black bodies—secure the possibility of familiarity. They support a necessary comfort that allows for dwelling, for rest, for orientation. And orientation is necessary. Earlier, I channeled Heidegger to state that dwelling is central to the subject's constitution. The one who can rest is the one who cannot help *but* rest. But in resting, the subject announces the fact that it is conditioned by the very matter upon which it rests in the first place.

In this regard, the religious and theodicean creation that is the accursed black body is more than an inescapable trap for the blackness consigned to it. It is also necessary for the one who did the cursing, for the one(s) who created and continue to carry out the corporeal maledictions in the first place. If religion is about "how one comes to terms with the ultimate significance of one's place in the world," then one cannot help but notice that the cursed black bodies that stand as available objects found and fund such coming to terms.[79] The one who wields the power of the corporeal malediction reaches for black bodies in order to create a dwelling and, in so doing, implicitly demonstrate black bodies as conditions of the subject's possibility.

No matter what Loehmann and Weekley and their supporters say or said, what is incontrovertibly true is that both Loehmann and Weekley became who they are through their infanticidal violence. Their violence shaped, formed, and announced them as subjects who defined notions of public safety and innocence. They may not have thought about this in the moment of encounter—in fact, chances are, they didn't. But whether or not they did, the incontrovertible fact is that they killed Tamir Rice and Aiyana

Stanley-Jones, and they justified their actions through a turn to their training or their circumstances.

Moreover, their (non)trials—like so many others—fashioned the public as a subjective space in need of black bodies to secure its comfort. The one who suggests that police are necessary, even if such a claim is obviated by discourses of reform, is—or at least attempts to be—a subject, deploying the corporeal malediction that curses black bodies as merely corporeal, necessary, no longer thinkable, and therefore unthought objects of their dwelling. The dwelling subject is already ultimately oriented, but such orientation works itself out, comes to terms with itself, through (sanctioning or tolerating) unthought violence enacted against unthought black bodies.

I highlight thoughtlessness because it's important to show how subjectivity is conditioned by something it will not or maybe even cannot fully capture through deliberation, through reason, through will. The subject is conditioned by something beyond thinking, something that calls to it from nowhere and everywhere, engendering its activity with and without its consent. It manifests itself as thoughtlessness, as absentmindedness; intention isn't (always) important. I'm sure both Weekley and Loehmann would claim that they are not racist. I'm sure they'd also claim that they didn't intend to kill children when they began their shifts those days. But they did it nonetheless. They did it without hesitation. Thoughtlessness occasions and announces dwelling. It provides (religious) orientation. It names familiarity. It provides rest. And it does so by sensing, cursing, using, and expending black *korper*.

Conclusion: Thoughtlessness as a Portal to the Beyond

The thoughtless engagement that reinforces black bodies as no-longer-thinkable objects of utilitarian concern conditions the dwelling subject. It announces that there is something beyond thought that makes the subject possible, that calls it into being. Situated beyond thought, thought about to be thought no longer, merely corporeal black bodies condition a form of violence to which they fall prey; they are conjured through a form of violence that is its own theodicean justification. Thoughtlessly killing, and then thoughtfully justifying this thoughtless killing, Weekley and Loehmann disclosed that they owe their existence to something beyond their cognitive and deliberative capacities.

While the beyond serves as a justification for the subject's violence, it is also—and nevertheless—an invitation. It is an opening, a reminder, that there is some dimension of materiality that refuses apprehension, exceeds thought's grasp, and therefore eludes cognitive and epistemological capture. This beyond highlights that Aiyana and Tamir's lives exceed the overdetermination of their bodies. They may have been killed because they were bodies, but they also lived as flesh—as moving, breathing, relational, loving, and lovable flesh.

I'll say more about this in chapter 2. For now, I will say this: to live as flesh is to already live beyond what Baby Suggs, Holy, called the "yonder," where black life isn't loved, where black bodies continue to circumscribe the appearance of black personhood. It is to know that exceeding thought will entail thoughtless violence; it is to see the yonder for what it is. But acknowledging one's existence as flesh also allows one to see possibility. It is to know that the violence of this world is not all there is.

Spillers provides the theoretical companion to this literary passage when she decides to make a distinction between the body and flesh, and ultimately argues that it is the flesh, not the body, that "registers the wounding" of overdetermination. For Spillers, the flesh is a "primary narrative," that which not only resists but feels; it is the flesh that is "seared, divided, and ripped apart"; it is the flesh that escapes overboard.[80] The accursed black body is already rendered captive, is already trapped, already given over to overdetermined captivity. But the flesh? Only yonder they flay it—which means there is something beyond the yonder, something that surpasses the yonder even as the yonder remains a threat. Morrison names the beyond as the clearing where Baby Suggs gave her sermon, and where flesh was validated and loved.

The clearing is not limited to fiction, and neither is it merely a spatiotemporal reality; the clearing—where flesh is loved and cared for, where flesh exists beyond the yonder of the body—can and will be brought along. Ashon Crawley makes this clear in *Blackpentecostal Breath*.

> Though the clearing is where [black people] would come together for sustenance, they would return to society civil, violent. But a return is not what they desired; they would have the logics—the spatial and temporal theological-philosophical thought that produced such illusory distinction—undone. But how are they able to gather, and gather quickly, in the midst of that which bears upon them? And we might ask this question of the nimbleness and quickness of gathering for residents of Ferguson, MO, responding to the murder of Mike Brown contemporarily. It means that even in civil society—even

under surveillances of cameras . . . they are always in the clearing,
they carry the clearing with them, enact the clearing.[81]

In the wake of Rice's and Stanley-Jones's deaths and the vindication of
their killers, people gathered as well—in much the same way they did
for Brown.[82] To live as flesh then is, as Weheliye says, to live an "alternate
instantiation of humanity that does not rest on the mirage of western Man
[that is, humanity and subjectivity as conceived as white and male] as the
mirror image of human life as such."[83] It is to scream "black lives matter"
knowing people may not listen.

Rice and Stanley-Jones may have been bodies, but they were also
flesh; and because they lived as flesh, other fleshy beings created clearings out of nowhere, revering, admiring, remembering, and loving their
flesh when they knew Detroit and Cleveland—and their respective police
departments—did not. "Hands may kill," Loehmann wrote in his police
report, and his did. His hands secured his and the public's vindication and
comfort. But Tamir's and Aiyana's hands, and the hands of others, were
and are loved. Even if this love does not signal the eradication or even
mitigation of antiblack violence, even if this love doesn't nullify the bodily
curse that is corporeal malediction, even if this love comes to the fore in
and through the very violence enacted in the yonder, we know—I know—
that flesh is still there, exceeding thought's demands and naming a horizon
of possibility that is irreducible to the categorical schemas that enact violence upon unthought and no-longer-thinkable black people. Baby Suggs
is right: *we flesh.* We always have been. We always will be.

"WHAT I DO?"
BLACK FLESH AS
LIVING MATTER

Who is to say where
outside begins & flesh ends? Perhaps we
are all just webs of blue information
intersecting, collapsing across strata

& calling it something else,
something other than entropy
or decay, a turf war with time.
So many names for breaking into this life

at angles unplanned & unknowable. It's true.
There is much to be praised in this house
of lightning & dust, this sloppy armor
we yearn to move more beautifully in.
                —Joshua Bennett, "On Flesh," in *The Sobbing School*

They came in two sets of three. Six staccato shots fired at point-blank range. The first set apparently wasn't enough; Blane Salamoni had to make sure.

> After the first three shots were fired, Officer Salamoni rolled onto his back, facing Sterling's back, with his weapon still drawn. Officer Lake stood behind both of them with his weapon drawn and pointed at Sterling. Sterling began to sit up and roll to his left, with his back to the officers. Sterling brought his right arm across his body toward the ground, and Officer Lake yelled at Sterling to "get on the ground." As Sterling continued to move, Officer Salamoni fired three more rounds into Sterling's back.[1]

If you've watched the videos, you notice how rapidly events unfold.[2] Four seconds in, Sterling is speaking to Lake; ninety seconds later, Sterling is no longer alive.[3] It happens so fast that you only have time to notice the obvious: the hands that grab and twist, the palms that grip pistol handles, the fingers that graze and pull triggers. You notice all the ways that the officers try to subdue Sterling with varying degrees of success. You notice, for example, that Lake is already touching Sterling, grabbing his arm to try to subdue him. You see Lake struggling mightily to push Sterling's arm down, and you see the officers twist Sterling's arms, pushing him down on the hood of the car. You see the officers struggle, you see Sterling struggle, you see . . . struggle.

You also hear struggle. You hear commands—or, rather, repetitions of the same command: "Don't move." Neither Salamoni nor his partner, Howie Lake II, tell Sterling why they are there, but they do command him to stop moving—and they do it within four seconds of Salamoni's arrival. First command: *Don't move, bruh, stop.*

Sterling speaks: "What I do?" he says. No answer. Salamoni is a man possessed; he points a gun to Sterling's head. Second command: *Don't move, or I'll shoot you in your fuckin' head!*

Salamoni's violence intensifies. He and Lake force Sterling onto the hood of a silver Toyota Camry. As Sterling moves and struggles, you hear the third command: *Don't fuckin' move or I'll shoot you in your fuckin' head!*

Sterling attempts to stand up. He keeps moving. His arms are somewhat straight until either Lake or Salamoni (the movement is out of the frame) moves his arm in an uncomfortable position. Sterling speaks again: "What I did, sir?"

Though the officers had initially subdued Sterling on the car, he somehow evades them—no kicking, no punching, just evasion. Fugitivity. Sterling stands up straight; Salamoni commands Lake to taser Sterling. The first one hits, and temporarily immobilizes him. But the second one misses, and Sterling stands up again. At this point, Salamoni has had enough. He tackles Sterling, slams him to the ground, and Officer Lake joins Salamoni in pinning Sterling down to the asphalt. While everyone is on the ground, Salamoni sees a gun. He's undone; Sterling "[broke] into this life at angles unplanned and unknowable," and Salamoni is at his wit's end. You hear him issue the fourth command, which has somehow also become a prayer: *You fuckin' move, I swear to God!*

But Sterling keeps moving. And it's too much. Salamoni is (dis)possessed. The shots ring out. Sterling seizes, and then his body relaxes. The blood pools. It's all over.

It all happens too fast—so fast that you miss things. It's hard to witness the moments when Sterling places his hands on the hood of the car to prop himself up or, while he's on the car, Sterling's head is turned upward, toward the body cam. You miss the moment before he's tased—when, while standing straight up, he extends his arms outward. And you certainly don't hear "What I do?" and "What I did?" It's hard to witness Sterling, to behold him. The officers occlude your view.

It's hard to see and hear Sterling because the obvious takes over, because the brackets have already been put in place. These aren't films, but they might as well be. They're set up for your investment (or perverse entertainment); they frame the contact in advance. Whether you think they were justified or not, your gaze is focused. It has been focused. It has been made to focus—on the officers. They are obvious. The obvious is already read, readily understood; it is steeped in assumptions; it traffics in presuppositions. It lays bare what we already know and what we're conditioned to know. The obvious presents the officers as the primary actors; Sterling is just the material by which they show themselves.

You therefore don't focus on Sterling because you can't; you're unaware that you've been made to view this video in a particular way. What has become second nature to you is not actually natural; what is obvious isn't the whole story.

The obvious doesn't capture everything that appears—that's what makes it obvious. Sterling appears. He's there, always there, moving and speaking. But the officers terminate your vision and crowd your hearing; you see and hear them. After watching the videos in this way, after having your focus trained on the obvious, you move to obvious conclusions. You've made up your mind: the officers are either heroes or villains, and conversely, Sterling is either a martyr or a monster—take your pick. In all of this, you fail to realize that you've missed Sterling himself, that you've made him into a martyr or a monster. You're undone. You don't return to the videos, but you reflect more deeply. And in your reflection, it hits you: you haven't the slightest clue what Sterling was doing.

* * *

Dear reader: I know this is hard. I know this is unsettling. But this is what sitting-with requires. I do not write this story to merely replay narratives of gratuitous violence. I write them because, if we sit with Sterling and not the officers, we begin to see different things. We begin to see things differently.

* * *

Apparently, the officers didn't know what Sterling was doing either—especially Blane Salamoni. He was so frantic that his version of events loses all credibility.

Salamoni alleges that he shot and kept shooting because Alton Sterling pointed a gun at him, but Lake tells a different story. "Lake recalled Sterling's demeanor differently," we're told; he "said he also never saw the man point a gun. He told Baton Rouge police that Sterling 'would not cooperate and listen to the commands that were given to him, but he did not punch or kick.'" Hell, the FBI isn't even convinced: "The evidence simply cannot establish . . . the position of Sterling's right hand at the exact time of the shooting," so the report says.[4] Salamoni couldn't get his story straight; Lake and the FBI say otherwise.

The truth, though, is that this isn't about them. It's about Sterling. I only bring up Salamoni's lies because they point us back to Sterling; while Salamoni, Lake, and the FBI disagree about the nature of the events, they all agree on two points: Sterling moved, and he spoke. That matters. That's what matters most.

In this chapter, I sit with Sterling. I attempt to hear and see Sterling. I listen to Sterling's illegible speech. I track Sterling's indeterminate movement. Hearing and seeing Sterling doesn't afford me conclusions about Sterling himself. I cannot tell you what Sterling meant by his speech and movement. But in sitting with him, I can expose the officers and their violence. I can disclose the meaning of their own speech and movements—the speech and movements of normative subjects.

By not interpreting Sterling's speech and movement, the officers show themselves as inept at encountering flesh without enacting violence. They edit his speech in an attempt to hail him on the page, but it backfires.

They ascribe motivation to his movements where it might not be, showing themselves to be out for blood. When flesh speaks unintelligibly, subjects attempt to interpret it. When it moves indeterminately, subjects ascribe motivations. Violence ensues. And sometimes, it's lethal.

Sterling spoke.

Sterling moved.

This chapter is about the excessive (non)meaning of Sterling's speech and movement.

Divine Duty: The Deonto(theo)logy of Threat

Sterling moved. And Sterling spoke. That means something. In fact, Sterling's speech and movement mean so much that they do not mean any-*thing*—which is to say, any specific thing. They are so supersaturated with possibility that one meaning won't fully capture what happened.

This is why he was threatening. Brian Massumi will tell us that the logic of threat is the double conditional: Sterling had a gun, and Sterling was speaking and moving, which meant that Sterling would have killed if he could.[5] Irrespective of any contrary evidence, speculation is more than enough to engender proactive violence. And this is precisely what the Louisiana Department of Justice claims.

> Even if the officers tried de-escalating the situation with Sterling by speaking with him, *the fact remained that no matter what Sterling said or did during his encounter with Salamoni and Lake, they believed he was armed with [a] firearm.* While the question Sterling posed to the officers asking them "What I do," could have been an example of him attempting to comply, it could also have been an example of Sterling using subterfuge in an attempt to convince the officers he was not a threat even though his intentions may have been otherwise. *While the video showed Sterling with his hands in the air, a possible sign he was giving up,* the officers had just experienced Sterling's continued resistance even when he was tased and had a firearm pointed at him.[6]

Salamoni confirms this: "There is no doubt in my mind not a single doubt that if I wouldn't have shot [Sterling], that me and Off. Lake would not be here today, because I know that Off. Lake was so close; [Sterling] would have easily shot [Lake] as well."[7] But the truth is Salamoni had to have doubt; we don't know what would have happened, because Salamoni cut short all possibility. Sterling spoke and he moved, but his movements and speech do not tell us his intentions. For Salamoni, though, it doesn't matter; if a black man moves, you shoot.[8]

In retrospect though, subjects do more thinking. Their logic mutates, and the double conditional becomes a fact: "would have, could have" becomes "when he did." That's what Baton Rouge Police Department (BRPD) detective R. Cook said anyway: "When the subject attempted to reach for the gun from his pockets the officers fired their police issued duty weapon at the subject to stop the threat."[9] Indeterminate movement becomes a double conditional, which becomes determined motivation—which means Salamoni did what he had to do. He killed because it was his deontological duty.

Salamoni didn't do his duty simply out of existential threat, though. God was on his side, too. Remember that the last command was a prayer: *I swear to God!* God was the guarantor of his being; God was the reason he was alive. "Salamoni credited God with saving his life, claiming Sterling had '100 percent' pointed a .38-caliber revolver at him while the two were wrestling on the ground. He said he used repeated profanity during and even after the encounter in part because he was 'so mad at Sterling for making him kill him,' according to police reports released Friday."[10] This is ontotheology at work.[11] But this is also deontology at work. Salamoni was carrying out his duties (deontology) as an agent of both the state and God (ontotheology)—which, in the end, amounts to the same thing.[12] Salamoni, therefore, was saved by doing his job, carrying out his divinely appointed law enforcement duties to protect his safety as well as the safety of the public. An ontotheological syllogism emerges: Sterling would have if he could have; God grounded Salamoni's being, and therefore equipped him with the tools to eliminate this double conditional; therefore, God was on Salamoni's side that day. That's how the ontotheologic works.[13]

Salamoni's deonto(theo)logical reasoning justifies his violence. Salamoni didn't know what Sterling was doing; that's why he repeated himself four times. But upon reflection, all the gaps are filled: not only was Sterling "reaching" for a gun, he was also pointing it at Salamoni. "Would have, could have" becomes "when he did," and a command—"Don't move"—retrospectively becomes clairvoyance: "There is no doubt in my mind . . . that if I wouldn't have shot . . . [we] would not be here today."[14] Salamoni clearly didn't know what Sterling was doing; he thought he already knew. No other possibilities were present.

Unruly Flesh

Sterling's speech and movement disclose a modality of black life that both conditions and exceeds the thinking subject. Sterling's actions on the day of his death signal a site of materiality that is always and already beyond the cognitive and subjective schemes of calculation, of reason, of thought: we call this site flesh, and I say *we* intentionally here.[15]

Sterling reminds us of flesh's possibilities. He reminds us of flesh's unruliness. Flesh weaves together contradictions, leaving them unresolved. It is both the site of Christological incarnation and the site of sinfulness.[16] It is the condition for loving relation as well as the effect of violence.[17] It holds itself out beyond the logics of this world while sustaining it. Flesh is nothing and everything. It is nothing *because* it is everything.

The contradictions shouldn't be surprising. Those who have heard and felt flesh know quite well that flesh is more (and less) than the philosophical logic of noncontradiction. Flesh asks more of the subject than what the subject can allow. As Hortense Spillers claims, flesh corresponds to a "liberated subject-position" whose ungendered presence *en*genders a series of inter- and transgenerational hieroglyphics that "come to be hidden to the cultural seeing by skin color."[18] And Maurice Merleau-Ponty tells us that "there is no name in philosophy" to describe flesh.[19] Those who have felt flesh know that it is unruly. They know that flesh exceeds rules, and subjects cannot abide flesh's unruliness. Violence ensues.

Sterling brings Spillers and Merleau-Ponty together. He expresses their shared conviction that, first, flesh conditions the body, and second, that flesh conditions relations with the world and others in it. Merleau-Ponty speaks of the flesh as that which is "the inauguration of the *where* and the *when*" as well as that which "makes the fact be a fact."[20] Spillers clues us into flesh's constitutive and generative role in relation to the body it founds: "Before the 'body,'" she writes, "there is the 'flesh,' that zero degree of social conceptualization that does not escape concealment under the brush of discourse, or the reflexes of iconography."[21]

Spillers and Merleau-Ponty agree that flesh is the body's condition of appearance. But there are differences. Unlike Merleau-Ponty, whose work "[drives home] . . . the fact that the flesh is primordially dehiscent" and therefore relies upon the social difference of bodies to disclose its operations, Spillers understands flesh as a "primary narrative," as that which "registers the wounding" of racialized and gendered violences that occasion the emergence of the body in the first place.[22] Bodies are captive. Bodies conform to rules. But flesh is unruly. Flesh exceeds rules, even as it sets them in sharp relief.

Sterling was unruly. He didn't fit. He doesn't fit. He couldn't fit. He didn't assent to juridical, metaphysical, or epistemological categories.[23] His movement exceeded the frame. No one knew—no one knows—the meaning of his movement. Salamoni's repeated command betrays his alleged certainty and surety: he repeated himself because he wasn't sure. *Don't move because I don't and can't know what your movement means.* He couldn't (over)determine what Sterling was trying to do as he stood and writhed on the ground. Sterling's struggle exceeded sense. He moved and spoke differently. He moved and spoke opaquely. He moved and spoke beyond what a subject knows and ever could know.

Sterling isn't mere source material. I do not simply apply Spillers and Merleau-Ponty—among others—to Sterling's case. After all, they do not read flesh. They sit with it. They listen to it. They trace its contours. Spillers speaks of fleshy hieroglyphics; Merleau-Ponty asks about flesh's touch. They do not determine flesh; they do not interpret it. But they do offer a way to sit with flesh, to sit with Sterling, to hear and see him.

Let us hear.

Hearing Sterling: The Call of Flesh

Sterling spoke, but he wasn't heard. Lake and Salamoni said and did nothing in response to his utterances. They moved irrespective of his speech. They didn't hear him. They couldn't hear him. It isn't that the officers were physically incapable of hearing Sterling. In fact, according to a BRPD internal investigation report, Salamoni clearly claims that he heard Sterling speak: "Off. Salamoni replied, 'He stated what did I do several times.'"[24] They knew he'd spoken; Sterling's speech just didn't register to them. Sterling literally, syntactically, and semantically said nothing, "nothing of consequence. Nothing of weight. Nothing of materiality."[25]

After all, "What I do?" and "What I did?" aren't proper questions—they're broken ones.[26] As broken questions, they break grammar—"What I do?" leaves out an auxiliary verb (What *did* I do?). In breaking grammar, they break grammar's rules—"What I did, sir?" misplaces the verb (What *did* I, sir?). And in breaking grammar's rules, they break open the rules—of grammar, of time, of space: "What I did, sir?" forces an ellipsis—"What did I . . . sir?" These nonquestions leave time and space open. They disrupt grammar's certainty. They leave one bereft of epistemological resources. Sterling spoke "gobbledygook"; his grammatically incorrect—which is to say, his grammatically disruptive—speech might as well have been pidgin.[27] Sterling spoke nothing—nothing but (which is to say, the nothingness of) noise.[28]

This isn't a grammar lesson. Sterling's speech is a fleshy and noisy catechism in nongrammar, an induction into the possibilities opened up by the voided space of broken nonquestions. "Noise *is*," Ashon Crawley tells us, "only insofar as it is irreducibly social, irreducibly formed by vibration off other surfaces, through and against air such that vibration, movement, begs its being heard, its being listened to."[29] In hearing Sterling, one can hear the "irreducible sociality" of Crawley's noise—a noise that exceeds and disrupts the attempt to try and understand Sterling's intentions.

To hear Sterling is to hear black flesh. It is to hear a mutation of proper English through disruptive and dissonant speech. Crawley reminds us that noise is something to be abated, something so disquieting that it invites silencing from external and categorical hearers.[30] The nothingness of noise, the nothingness that is noise, invites violence. It invites the violence of correction. Salamoni corrects Sterling's grammar in his recollection of events: "What I do?" becomes "What *did* I do?" The correction is in place, and it mirrors the physical violence of correction that occurred in the parking lot.

If Crawley articulates noise as that which militates against, is allergic to, and yet visited by, the violence of categorical distinctions, then it might be possible to hear Fred Moten's reading of "pidgin," of "gobbledygook," as an expression of the irreducibly social noise Crawley breathes through his own writing.[31] Against and beyond the normative claims of the linguistic "standard" that Frantz Fanon struggles to exorcise from his own thinking, Moten hears pidgin's linguistic distortion as possibility. The deformation is, yes, a deformation—and is treated as such—but this deformation is also possibility, steeped in and birthed from a "dispossessive fleshliness that corresponds to the fullest possible understanding of . . . a nothingness without reserve independent of the desire to show up in and for the conventional optics wherein somebody is delineated and identified."[32]

Inverse Interpellation: Flesh's Call

In sitting with the poetics and poiesis of Sterling's pidgin speech, in hearing the nonsensical noise of nothingness that Sterling spoke, we can (and cannot help but) hear flesh—and particularly, we can (and cannot help but) hear flesh's disregard for the "conventional optics" that would hail it as a subject.[33] Sterling was hailed, but the hailing didn't take. Sterling identified himself, but not from within the state's normative terms. His "I" was not a proper grammatical or political subject.

The "I" in "What I do?" and "What I did, sir?" is not an acknowledgment; it "undermines the capacity to 'be' in a self-identical sense."[34] "What I do?" and "What I did, sir?" do not announce Sterling as guilty or innocent before the law. They cannot be understood and therefore identified. They are disruptive nonquestion(ing)s that refuse the logic of interpellation. To hear Sterling is to hear fragments uttered in the interrogative. It is to hear brokenness. It is to hear broken English. It is to hear English broken open.

Breaking English open, Sterling left the officers at a linguistic and hermeneutic loss; they could not make sense of Sterling's utterances, and therefore ignored them. They did not converse with Sterling. But this is because they couldn't. Sterling broke English open, and in doing so, nullified the possibility of intersubjective recognition. Sterling broke open the grammatical terms by which the norm would announce itself and enforce its authority. Sterling destroyed the possibility of conversation—and therefore made recognition impossible. The officers could identify Sterling. But that's all they could do. "Off. Salamoni stated that he observed Off. Lake walking toward a b/m [black male] subject wearing a red t-shirt, who appeared to be standing next to a Cd stand outside of the said business. This subject was later identified as ALTON STERLING."[35] Identifying Sterling, they couldn't think him: Salamoni frantically (and maybe neurotically) repeated himself. Lake fell silent.

This doesn't mean that subjects won't still try to think, to re-cognize what they see and hear. Subjects will fill in the gaps. They'll correct what wasn't in need of correction. They'll siphon intelligibility from unintelligible excess.

BRPD INTERNAL AFFAIRS: Do you remember the statements Sterling was making at the time?

SALAMONI: He stated what did I do several times. Off. Lake told him to put his hands on the car, in which time I became aggressive stating hey you better listen.[36]

Salamoni remembered Sterling saying "What *did* I do?," filling in the gaps and therefore turning a nonquestion into a proper question.

We might want to see this grammatical correction as immaterial to the violence Salamoni enacted.[37] But I want to suggest that Salamoni "fixed" Sterling's "English" in the same way that he lethally "fixed" Sterling as a corpse through the pulling of a trigger. Salamoni's grammatical corrections mirror his role as an officer who brings correction by enforcing the law. Speaking illegibly, Sterling called the officers into being as self-identifying subjects, as subjects of and for the law. As subjects of and for the law, the officers were unwilling and unable to leave the noisy poetics of Sterling's pidgin speech unmolested.

Think about it: had Sterling actually asked Salamoni's question, he'd have spoken the linguistic justification for his own demise. Had Sterling actually said, "What *did* I do?," then the officers would have gained a grammatical ground that would have only reinforced the logic of guilt and innocence that attends interpellation. "What did I do?" can still be read as disobedience to the law—even if this disobedience occurs through questioning. Sterling would therefore be grammatically subject to the law's terms, legitimating the law's authority—and announcing himself as "really" the legal subject (able to be) guilty before the law.[38] The proper question, therefore, doesn't assuage the suspicion; it only reinforces it. Proper questions can be answered, even if these answers are assumed. Had Sterling asked this question, all Salamoni would have had to do—and all he did anyway—was record Sterling's question(ing) as disobedience, and call it a day.

But Sterling didn't ask that question, which means that Salamoni didn't record Sterling's speech. Sterling didn't ask a question at all (again, I am not attempting to distill any meaning from Sterling's speech itself). But by filling in the gaps, by fixing Sterling's grammar, Salamoni exposed himself as hearing disobedience where it might not have been. The proper question can still come off as a threat. But the nonquestion, irrespective of Salamoni's re(d)actions (and Sterling's intentions, for that matter), is neither refusal nor acquiescence. Uttering an alien tongue, Sterling dislodged the certainty of his alleged guilt.[39] No longer certain, Salamoni fixed Sterling's claims in the name of (divine) order. No wonder Salamoni thanked God for killing Sterling.

But, divine in(ter)ventions notwithstanding, it wasn't Salamoni's God who called him into being. Salamoni didn't (re)gain his sense of selfhood through God, but instead through his inability to understand Sterling's irreducibly illegible speech. By asking nonquestions, by uttering speech that was irreducible to the constriction of grammatical norms, Sterling hailed *the officers*. He called *them* into being as the ones beholden to (executing) the law. The complainant may have brought them to the scene, but Sterling confirmed them as the executives (and executors) of the law.

UNION ATTORNEY CHRISTOPHER SONNIER: Did that uniform clearly identify you as a police officer and would anyone that encountered you would have any doubt that you were a police officer?

SALAMONI: I was clearly identified as a police officer and there would have been no doubt that I was a police officer.[40]

Hearing Sterling, then, doesn't show Sterling as the one who was hailed. Quite the opposite—or the inverse: the law is hailed from something beyond the law, something that exceeds the law. The law is hailed by something that doesn't simply break the law but breaks it open. Having been fractured, the law needs an individual who can restore it. And this individual, happy to oblige the law, becomes a subject by eliminating the excess in the name of the law that the excess broke open. The self-identifying individual—which is to say, the subject—then, is not the one who (allegedly) transgresses the law, but instead the one who restores it by exemplifying, embodying, and executing it.

STERLING: What I did, sir?

SALAMONI: [It really is me!] Don't fuckin' move or I'll shoot you in your fuckin' head![41]

Salamoni's God might be the one who "saved" him, but, on that day, Salamoni's God was not the condition for his subjectivity. Sterling was.

To hear Sterling, then, is to hear the (re)birth of the subject through redaction. To hear Sterling is to hear the subject attempt to gain its own footing by correcting speech according to the norms of its own making. Reacting to Sterling's speech, Lake and Salamoni exposed themselves as subjects who cannot help but live, move, and have their being in and through violent and coercive correction.

Instead of articulating Sterling as the individual in need of guilty subject formation, Sterling's fleshy linguistic rupture exposes Salamoni and Lake as individuals in desperate need of subjectivity through lethal execution in the name of the law. The one who is invested in trying to make Sterling's speech "work" is the one who remains preoccupied with order; the one who cannot suffer pidgin speech is the one who forms as a subject through the elimination of such noisy utterances.

To hear Sterling is to hear flesh speak to, beyond, and against the subjects it cannot help but make possible. The one who cannot help but correct Sterling's speech—the one who cannot resist quenching their thirst for intelligibility—is the one who self-identifies as the subject violently formed out of the expressive plenitude that is black flesh. Sterling spoke—illegibly. And this illegibility couldn't be left alone. Sterling's speech is a fleshy catechism in inverse interpellation. And Salamoni's (neurotic) reiterations of "Don't move!" were catechetical recitations.

The recitations were dramatic. They were loud. They were uttered with increasing intensity. They got louder. The velocity and volume with which Salamoni spat his words increased with every moment, with every act of avoidance, with every refusal that was not a refusal—and yet could not help but be read as one. Sterling called, and the officers responded. Sterling spoke, and the officers interpreted. Violently.

Seeing Sterling: The Movement and Touch of Flesh

Sterling also moved. And every time he moved, "Don't move!" gained steam. It increased its threatening velocity with every muscle spasm, with every jerk, every roll, every step, every movement that Sterling made. The officers expressed their desire to siphon intelligibility from unintelligible movement.[42] Unable to hear Sterling, they made Sterling's movement the evidence for threatening and malicious intent.

Sterling's first move was a turn. But not the turn of interpellation. Louis Althusser tells us that the hailed individual becomes a subject when they turn toward the law.[43] But when the officers came on the scene, Sterling didn't turn toward them. He placed the logic of interpellation in default.

> INTERNAL AFFAIRS: What was Sterling [sic] actions after you gave him that verbal command?
>
> LAKE: He kind of turned and tensed up and refused to turn towards the car. He actually turned away from the car towards the building.[44]

Sterling didn't self-identify as the suspect in need of subjectivation. This isn't disobedience—in fact it couldn't be: Sterling was never advised as to why he was the officers' target in the first place.

> INTERNAL AFFAIRS: Was Sterling ever advised of the reason why contact was made with him?
>
> LAKE: No sir he immediately started fighting, so we tried to take control of the situation.[45]

The officers never "advised [Sterling] of the reason why contact was made." (And, according to the Louisiana Department of Justice, the officers didn't have to.)[46] Sterling turned away. In turning away, he didn't submit. He didn't submit to a law he didn't even know he'd broken.

No worries. Sterling didn't need to be aware. He didn't need to think—in fact, he was never given the option to do so. Moving—turning (away)—was enough. The turning away was read as a refusal to comply, and this initial turning was more than enough to start a short but brutal scene of violent subject formation.

The officers would have us believe that Sterling would still be alive had he just stopped moving. But the cessation of movement is death. Sterling kept moving because he was still alive, which means that the more he moved, the more of a threat he became. Or at least this is what the officers would have us believe.

UNION ATTORNEY CHRISTOPHER SONNIER: At any point in time when Alton Sterling was on the ground, did he state that he would comply or did he stop moving?

SALAMONI: No sir he was constantly moving and kicking his legs. . . .

SONNIER: Why did you fire your weapon a second time?

SALAMONI: Because the suspect got up again and I thought my life was in danger when he started to pull a gun out of his pocket and turn towards me. I thought for sure I was going to die, I was laying on the ground and I had nowhere to go. I knew if he turned towards me with the pistol, he was going to kill me.[47]

Sterling moved after being shot; Salamoni assumed he was going for a gun. Salamoni concluded Sterling was reaching, and this "knowledge" compelled Salamoni to kill. Let Salamoni tell it, Sterling was so aggressive that there were no other options but lethal violence.

Salamoni killed Sterling, then, because he claims to have had no other options. And, as was noted earlier, this compulsion was steeped in religious language and ideas. "I like to think he was a devil," was how Salamoni put it.[48] And this "devil" "100 percent" pointed a gun at him. Bracketing all other possibilities, Salamoni went to what he already knew was the thing itself. He'd found Sterling's essence. Sterling was devilish. Sterling was a threat. Sterling kept moving. That couldn't change.

Lake didn't call Sterling a "devil," but Sterling might as well have been. According to Lake, when he deployed a taser on Sterling, "[Sterling] didn't even flinch."[49] Electricity wasn't effective, so Lake concluded the same thing that Salamoni did:

> INTERNAL AFFAIRS: Do you feel there was any other force other than lethal force, that could have been used in this incident?
>
> LAKE: We used everything. No sir.[50]

There was nothing they could have done. Sterling didn't flinch when the taser hit, and he got back up after he was shot the first three times. Sterling kept moving throughout the incident, and, just like his homicidal partner, Lake swore:

> INTERNAL AFFAIRS: When you pointed your weapon towards Sterling, did you give him any commands?
>
> LAKE: I said hey bruh if you fucking move I swear to God.[51]

Confronted with what might as well have been a demonic or even devilish entity, both Lake and Salamoni swore to their God before enacting homicidal violence. They agree: Sterling kept moving, so there was nothing else they could have done.

Despite their agreements about the implications of Sterling's movements, there is a slippage: Salamoni says Sterling pointed a gun, while Lake claims that Sterling never pointed a gun or expressed intentions to shoot anyone. Salamoni claimed that Sterling was punching and kicking; Lake claimed Sterling "wasn't swinging, punching, and kicking."[52] Where Salamoni saw threat, Lake saw refusal. They disagree. And they disagree because Sterling's movement could not be fully understood.

This isn't limited to Salamoni and Lake, either. In the introduction to this chapter, the FBI described the movement with less certainty. In the FBI's press release, there was no "reaching" language. All we know is that Sterling "began to sit up and roll to his left"—which is ironic, because, unless the videos are selfies, the gun was in Sterling's right pocket—and further describes Sterling's movement as bringing his "right arm across his body toward the ground" (which means, again, that Sterling was moving his right arm to his left side, nowhere near the gun in his right pocket). Not only does the FBI refrain from interpreting Sterling's movement; the bureau claims that Sterling moved in a different direction—away from the gun. The videos remain unclear; Sterling's movement remains open, lost to us after the six bullets pierced him.

But even the FBI's "restraint" is a reduction—one steeped in the violence of the law. The bureau's refrain is nothing less and nothing more than an attempt to hide behind reasonable doubt: "The evidence in this case," the release states, "is insufficient to bear the heavy burden of proof under federal criminal civil rights law."[53] And if this statement isn't enough, the FBI clarifies later on: "The evidence gathered during this investigation is insufficient to prove, beyond a reasonable doubt, that the use of force leading up to and including the shooting violated the Fourth Amendment."[54] Using the law as its shield, the FBI establishes the appropriateness of Salamoni and Lake's actions. The law offers no reprieve, no opportunity for redress; it used Sterling as equipment to secure the officers' innocence.[55] None of the videos provide clarity regarding Sterling's intentions, and the FBI uses this lack of clarity as a tool of vindication.

Uncertainty might be what got the officers off—locally and federally. But the "truer word" is that the officers killed Sterling because they wanted certainty. They didn't know what Sterling was doing; they were at a loss. Left to their own devices, they made a reactionary interpretive decision "to force enclosure, to create a boundary, to produce . . . a liberal subject, the possessive individual, through violence."[56] Sterling's physical movement operates as a form of "resistance that is prior to power," prior to the very possibility of embodied overdetermination itself.[57] Sterling moved as flesh. And that fleshy movement exceeds any of our frames of reference.

Pinning as Bracketing: Phenomenological Implications

That's the problem with (and promise of) flesh. It's messy. It doesn't submit. It isn't legible. Flesh "is not matter, is not mind, is not substance."[58] It refuses to play the political and ontological games of the subject. As such, the subject wrestles flesh to the ground. Subjects pin flesh down. They attempt to subdue flesh. They pierce flesh with their tools. They carve bodies—corpses—out of it. Attempting to (re)gain footing, subjects pin the plenitude of indeterminate flesh down into the motivations of a body.

When Sterling moved, the officers came closer. They didn't leave him alone. The "refusal to comply" brought them in closer proximity with Sterling. Salamoni eventually tackled him, and Lake joined in. They were on the ground. They pinned him down.

This is the case because subjects cannot help but be phenomenological subjects. They need objects; they desire order. They strive toward certainty. Flesh isn't an object; it must be made into one—which is to say, it must be cursed by corporeal maledictions. It must undergo reduction; it needs to be bracketed.

Edmund Husserl may have wanted to leave presuppositions behind. But his method, his scientific philosophy, strove toward indubitable proof. Husserl's phenomenological subject strives toward a certainty that it may not be able to achieve but nevertheless cannot do without. The subject needs evidence to carry out its investigations; it relies upon the clear certainty of the thing itself to make its claims.

It might be hard to hear Husserl whispering through the investigation, but he's there. Listen: "Any evidence is a grasping of something itself . . . with full certainty of its being, certainty that accordingly excludes every doubt."[59] And now listen to the investigation:

> INTERNAL AFFAIRS: Could you tell me if the weapon was pointed at you at any time?
>
> SALAMONI: 100% it was pointed at me [*full certainty*], we were laying belly to belly and the gun was pointed straight towards [my] thighs and groin.[60]
>
> INTERNAL AFFAIRS: Did you put both of your hands on Alton Sterling's hand or on the revolver?
>
> SALAMONI: On his hand but I could feel the coldness of the revolver. . . . I knew for sure what I felt was a gun [*excludes every doubt*].[61]
>
> INTERNAL AFFAIRS: Did Sterling fit the description of the information provided to you by headquarters?
>
> SALAMONI: Yes sir 100% [*full certainty*]. . . . [62]
>
> UNION ATTORNEY CHRISTOPHER SONNIER: If Sterling would have fired his weapon while it was still in his pocket, in your mind you feel it still would have hit you correct?
>
> SALAMONI: Yes 100% [*excludes every doubt*].[63]

There was no doubt in Salamoni's mind that Sterling was the man they were looking for, that Sterling's gun was pointed at him, that Sterling would have hit him had Sterling shot the gun. In confirming everything "100%," Husserl's desperate desire for certainty resonates in and through Salamoni's claims.

Husserl would want to disagree, though. He'd suggest that this isn't quite apodictic evidence. He'd be right, of course. But Salamoni's "100%" *lays claim* to apodicticity. Even if Salamoni's perspective was only adequate evidence, it was nevertheless taken to be true. It was more than enough to solidify Salamoni's vindication. The thinking subject doesn't need a high burden of proof to establish its certainty. It only needs to be certain. Its certainty is its evidence.

Husserl tells us that bracketing loses "all the formations pertaining to sociality and culture."[64] He suggests that the brackets make "the whole concrete surrounding life-world . . . for me, from now on, only a phenomenon of being, instead of something that is."[65] But this bracketing doesn't displace the subject's primacy. In fact, it further sediments the primacy of the subject. Once the subject becomes certain ("100%"), what were once appearances become expressions of truth—of truth for the subject itself. Listen (again):

> No matter what the status of this phenomenon's claim to actuality and no matter whether, at some future time, I decide critically that the world exists or that it is an illusion, still this phenomenon, itself *as mine*, is not nothing but is *precisely what makes such critical decisions at all possible and accordingly makes possible whatever has for me sense and validity as "true" being—definitively decided or definitively decideable being.*[66]

Bracketing is the way the subject (re)gains control. Husserl might want these merely subjective states to be grounded in something larger: he attempted this by thinking about the intersubjective world. But this all stems from the primacy of the subject, from the subject who demands that it be primary. Husserl's work is sourced by a normative assumption about who can be deemed a subject.

Husserl, therefore, traffics in the obvious. He sees what he's supposed to see. He sees the officers first. He misses Sterling's movements. He sees the subject as primary, but this is because he cannot see it any other way. He falls prey to his own machinations; subjects cannot abide by the messiness of the natural attitude.

But flesh displaces all of this. When it moves, it reinstates doubt (*Don't move, or I swear to God!*). Moving flesh reinforces the possibility that the subject might, indeed, be wrong—and, more importantly, rather irrelevant—in the space of concrete experience. Flesh offers no evidence—apodictic or otherwise. Flesh refuses adequation; it doesn't conform. Moving flesh forces the subject to repeat itself, incessantly and confusingly re-"introducing" itself in the "initiating moments" of violence it enacts.[67]

Indeterminate movement makes no sense; it allows for no conclusions. It leaves the subject stuck in the dirty mess of the natural attitude. For the thinking subject, movement needs direction. Movement has to aim toward something.[68] Movement must have a signification. It must tell the subject something—it must be, or become, intelligible. It must be subsumed into a system of signs, whereby the subject is called to interpret them.[69] For the subject, movement must be endowed with intention, with motivation. It must carry within it a discrete and transparent arc, pointing toward a goal— whether shared or not—that would terminate it. It must be pinned down.

Subjects pin (down). Salamoni and Lake pinned Sterling down. Subjects set up parameters. They predict in advance. Salamoni claimed that he was afraid for "pretty much the entire incident . . . because I knew there was a high probability that he was armed with a firearm."[70] He was ready for flesh's touch. This world was his. He already knew what Sterling was, what Sterling could be. Salamoni was ready. And he responded with a pin.

Pinning is the *epoché* in action. Pinning brackets. It suspends all other possibilities; it withholds judgments about what could be in favor of what one already knows. It doesn't leave presuppositions by the wayside—in fact, it relies upon them. One suspends judgment about reality because reality is messy.

Brackets clean up the mess; pinning down is thought's material strategy, and this—*this*—is how flesh splits, how flesh emerges as bodies, how flesh shows up in the world through violence. Flesh gets pinned. (Sterling was pinned.) And when it does, we begin to see "the calculated work of iron, whips, chains, knives, the canine patrol, the bullet" as the occasion for flesh's "dehiscence or fission of its own mass."[71] They came in two sets of three.

The Intimate, Dispossessive, and Prepossessive Touch of Flesh

The officers killed Sterling up close—they were "belly to belly" with him.[72] They enacted violence in the intimate and indeterminate space of moving flesh against moving flesh. There, *not* punching, kicking, or swinging is nevertheless read as fighting or as the possibility of lethal retaliation. It was something that had to be felt, something that could only be perceived through touch.

Flesh expresses itself through touch. Flesh calls us close. It invites proximity. And in inviting proximity, flesh is vulnerable. Merleau-Ponty wanted touch to expose a "pre-established harmony"; his meditations take us to a place of romance, of care. But he also knew that flesh could wound, that flesh "suffers when it is wounded."[73] They could feel him tense up. Touch was the condition of and for violence; it was the conduit through which Sterling was killed. One cannot "sear, divide, or rip-apart" flesh at a distance.[74] Sterling was touching the officers. They, in turn, were touching Sterling. They felt Sterling moving beneath them. In feeling Sterling move, they were moved.

Not of themselves. To be touched by flesh is to be dispossessed; it is to be disoriented and displaced. Flesh dispossesses subjects, displacing their centrality. Touch dissolves subjects; it makes them no longer relevant. Flesh's touch necessarily disorients "a subject-centered account," calling the subject and its centrality into question.[75] Touch robs subjects of their share. It divests them of their (illegitimate) claim to primacy. It reminds subjects that they owe their existence to something beyond themselves.

But flesh also prepossesses subjects to enact lethal violence. The one "who sees cannot possess the visible unless he [sic] is possessed by it," and, unable to endure its own displacement, the subject responds.[76] Salamoni told "internal investigators he had no choice but to open fire to save the lives of Lake and other civilians," rationalizing that the reason why "he used repeated profanity during and even after the encounter [was] in part because he was 'so mad at Sterling for making him kill him.'"[77]

The officers didn't move on their own accord; they were moved because they were "occasioned by alterity." Their animation came from beyond themselves, from the touch of an-other.[78] The subject doesn't find itself through its own self-consciousness, but instead through being touched by speaking and moving flesh.[79] Reason stems from a "relation of tactility," and this relation prompts the subject to act, and enact violence.

Flesh's dispossessive and prepossessive touch is vulnerable. It dissolves the subject through its own dissolution.[80] Flesh is dispossessed by the very prepossessive dispossession it enacts; it falls apart at the very moment it takes hold of the subject. Merleau-Ponty used the term "element" to get at it and, as Butler elaborates, highlighting flesh's expression and movement in this world as one of dissolution, of "coming apart."

Butler admits that they cannot figure out why flesh dominates through splitting.[81] Flesh cannot be theorized. Flesh comes from a dark place, from a place beyond the light of phenomenology, beyond the light of reason, beyond the (blinding) light of thought. Subjects can only *feel* flesh. In place of describing flesh, they describe their feelings. And, having described what they felt, subjects cognize their feelings. They turn tensing into fighting.

Though it doesn't come from the light, flesh is nevertheless forced to appear in the light. And flesh makes its appearance as split, broken apart, broken open through violent touches. Flesh appears through "the anatomical specifications of rupture," through "eyes beaten out, backs, skulls branded, a left jaw, a right ankle, punctured."[82] These ruptures are evidence of flesh's splitting. Splitting isn't soothing. Dehiscence isn't delicate. To subjects, flesh—and particularly black flesh—appears already dissected, already pulled apart into bodies, situated within the realm of brute corporeality.

BLACK FLESH: THE VIOLENT COMPULSION OF THE SUBJECT

This is why Spillers is necessary. Merleau-Ponty might discuss flesh's touch, but Spillers describes how black flesh doesn't voluntarily sediment into living bodies. It doesn't merely "become" a "being of two leaves," sentient and sensed.[83] One of the leaves falls away, leaving black *korper* as material residue. Though touch is Merleau-Ponty's primary word, he misses the fact that all touches are not the same, that pinning is also a form of touching, that "belly to belly" contact is an occasion for lethal violence. The officers were looking for a corpse, and they found one. They carved it out of Sterling's breathing, writhing, wriggling, and grunting flesh by subduing it, pinning it down, shooting it, touching it.

Sterling shows that black flesh is felt differently. Black flesh cannot be left unmolested. Its indecipherability is read as a puzzle or a problem to be solved. Adjusting to the world as flesh, Sterling struggled against the officers' acts to constrain him, to force him into a body. The birth of the subject comes through contact with black flesh, with feeling and being touched by the "concentration of ethnicity that contemporary critical discourses neither acknowledge nor discourse away."[84] But this touch is not taken as an invitation. It is taken as a challenge. Moving and tactile flesh constitute a challenge to the subject. And in so doing, it constitutes the subject itself.

Though flesh sits at the vestibule of the normative world, Sterling shows that black flesh appears in the world as an "irresistible and destructive sensuality."[85] Violence is the thinking subject's birthright and its legacy. It is the subject's heritage and its future. And this violence is enacted against and on matter—living matter, irresistible matter, matter that cannot help but be violently touched and pinned. Sterling spoke. Sterling moved. And in so doing, Sterling called the officers close. But their response to this call was nothing less than an assault—re(d)active in its structure, intimate in its scope, and nonconsensual in its relation.

Sterling shows that flesh conditions the subject through compulsion.[86] Subjects are compelled to enact violence: they edit flesh's speech; they violently bracket flesh's movement. Sterling's speech called the officers into being by calling them into question; the officers couldn't understand him, so they edited him instead. Sterling's movement and his touch constituted a challenge; the officers couldn't determine the meaning of his movements, so they drew closer and drew their guns instead. They enacted violence in the name of understanding. They killed in the name of reason.

The subject's violence against black flesh is excessive. The first three shots weren't enough. This is the case because subjects are compelled to enact excessive violence: "I felt that Alton Sterling made me do this," Salamoni claimed. "I didn't want to take his life. It was just an outpour of emotions, I had to kill somebody and I didn't want to do it so I guess I was frustrated."[87] He "had to kill somebody." He "was frustrated." He cussed as "an outpour of emotions." His violent language mirrored the violence he'd just enacted. And Lake felt the same way. Lake called Sterling "a fucking idiot because . . . [Sterling] made it go that way. Sterling could have just surrendered his hands and went back to jail."[88]

Though they disagree about what Sterling actually did, both of them were compelled to use lethal violence. They were prepossessed by black flesh's dispossessive touch; they were called close because of black flesh's unintelligible speech. And, as was the case with chapter 1, Salamoni and Lake are not alone. Jeronimo Yanez couldn't hear Philando Castile, and he shot excessively, killing him on camera. Lacquan MacDonald was shot sixteen times because he was walking. All of these men were armed. But the excessiveness with which the officers shot them came from a compulsory impulse.

Lake and Salamoni (say they) didn't want to kill Sterling. They say that wasn't their intention. But they did it anyway: Sterling was speaking unintelligibly, moving indeterminately, and dispossessively rubbing against them as they subdued him. This wasn't their fault; they couldn't help themselves. They couldn't help but shoot multiple times. They were compelled. They were called to kill.

EXCURSUS: FLESH'S BEYOND

To see Sterling move, then, is to see black flesh in action. It is to see flesh lived out, to catch a glimpse of black flesh's (primary) capacity to register wounding, to feel the brunt of the violence of this world. To sit with

Sterling is not to interpret him. It is to see how Sterling's obscurity, how his indeterminate, indecipherable, and irreducible speech and movement cannot be left alone. Sterling shows us that the subjectivity of the subject shows itself as helplessness, as a repetitive and fatalistic compulsion toward violence. Sterling's movement shows us that the subject emerges as a being for whom violence—the violence of correction, the violence of pinning, the violence of thought—is necessary to its founding and its sustenance. Sterling shows us that the subject's touch cannot help but be a pin, that the subject only makes contact through (lethal) constraint.

We might want to see the officers as one-offs. But they aren't the singularity here—Sterling is. The officers' actions aren't unique. And neither are their recollections. Invoking fear in the face of black flesh is a tried and true move in the affective economy of antiblackness. We know this to be the case because, again turning to Warren, the law substantiates the subject's violent birthright.[89] The law is the tool by which black flesh becomes black bodies. It is wielded in order to legitimate the act of constraining black life, of putting it in brackets. *Graham v. Connor*, reasonable doubt, stand your ground, and other laws turn the violence of the thinking subject into appropriate and proper behavior.[90] Though Sterling's movement and speech remain free of interpretation, expressing Sterling as singular and singularly excessive, the officers' actions are banal, quotidian. They are the stuff of the everyday. They are steeped in maintaining the average everydayness of subjects who cannot suffer indeterminate flesh.

Do not think of the officers as different from the normative Western subject. Do not think that their excessive violence is beyond the pale. Achille Mbembe already told us that one of the first words about blackness was its monstrosity, its phobogenic capacities.[91] Do not miss the utterly quotidian nature of their actions and their memories. Do not assume they're worse than those who do not wear their uniforms, or that their actions are abnormal, that they're anomalies freed of the violent logic of liberal subject formation in the West. Subjects have *been* afraid of black flesh. They have *been* enacting excessive violence against black flesh, splitting it for their own ends and fissuring it to justify their own modes of engagement. Salamoni and Lake's actions aren't aberrations. They're *expressions* of thought, physical and verbal articulations of the thinking subject who is compelled to violence in the face of excessive flesh.

But, as Alexander Weheliye once wrote, flesh is both the foundation for and dissolution of this normative world, this world of thinking subjects.[92] Weheliye correlated flesh to bare life, situating it as both supplement and constitutive outside. Flesh operates in and as the vestibule; its alterity comes from within. Sterling moved in ways that indicated his "liberated subject-position," and though this movement didn't liberate Sterling from the violence of this world, it nevertheless indicated something beyond this violence. I do not know what Sterling meant to do. He moved too much; his movement was full of possibility, of infinite indeterminacy. And it is precisely in that possibility that we can hear and see something beyond the violence of the thinking subject.

The beyond, the place where flesh weeps, laughs, and dances, is the space where love is possible, where flesh—where black flesh—shows itself as primary. It is the place where proper grammar isn't necessary: "we flesh." And it is the place where "moaning and groaning" isn't the condition for guilt, but instead the expression of release. Laugh. Dance. Cry. For the living and the dead. Just cry.

This beyond isn't magical, though. Although there is love in the beyond—though love constitutes the beyond—it isn't romanticized. Or at least it shouldn't be. It isn't pure. It isn't metaphysical. It isn't somewhere else; it is here—it has *been* here. The beyond doesn't fully escape the violence of the world of subjects (even as it sets it in sharp relief). But even as it doesn't fully avoid the world's violence, it nevertheless offers something else. Right here, and right now, and right alongside the brutality of thinking subjects.

The Beyond—the Clearing

The beyond traffics in otherwise possibilities. It erupts in the wake. It shows up as terrible beauty, embracing and highlighting unremarked yet remarkably wayward lives.[93] It is everywhere and nowhere, erupting from within, yet resonating and calling (from) beyond the violence that is this world. The beyond is "a place out of which emerges neither self-consciousness nor knowledge of the other but an improvisation that proceeds from somewhere on the other side of an unasked question."[94] Beyond shows itself in hush harbors and corners, erupting in alleys and at dinner tables, finding expression on streets and in jails. Beyond is the brush, the forest, the clearing—the Clearing. "When warm weather came, Baby Suggs, holy, followed by every black man, woman and child who could make it through, took her great heart to the Clearing—a wide-open place cut deep in the woods nobody knew for what at the end of a path known only to deer and whoever cleared the land in the first place."[95] *Nobody knew for what.* The

Clearing is not a space steeped in purposiveness. Intention didn't matter; what matters is they gathered—for collective release. In the beyond that was the Clearing, they expressed the freedom they always were and always had.

Expression is crucial.[96] Aside from Baby Suggs's words, language was unnecessary; laughter, dance, and tears were more than enough. Baby Suggs didn't simply speak; she called. She called them close. They came. But they didn't close in. They just came closer.

> She shouted, "Let the children come!" and they ran from the trees toward her.
>
> "Let your mothers hear you laugh," she told them, and the woods rang. The adults looked on and could not help smiling.
>
> Then "Let the grown men come," she shouted. They stepped out one by one from among the ringing trees.
>
> "Let your wives and your children see you dance," she told them, and groundlife shuddered under their feet.
>
> Finally she called the women to her. "Cry," she told them. "For the living and the dead. Just cry." And without covering their eyes the women let loose.[97]

They let loose. They shook the ground. The woods rang. Called close, they left their words in the trees. They didn't need (proper) speech; laughter, tears, and dance engendered a collective and connective release that did not need the correction awaiting them in the yonder.

If you don't think the Clearing is real, consider it: they came—thousands of them. They gathered—in front of the store where he died, in the stadium at Southern University in Baton Rouge—in his name, in the wake of the violence visited upon him. They gathered to laugh, dance, and cry—yes, for the dead, but as an homage to Sterling's life.[98] They moved—collectively. They sang illegible songs and shouted illegible chants. They moved in harmony and discord. Groundlife shuddered; they rang their surroundings. Sterling's flesh called thousands close; anyone who could and would "make it through" found their way to Baton Rouge. *Let them come.*

They came—in celebration, in protest. They may have even come to protest *as* celebration. After all, as Fred Moten intimates, "That we have to celebrate is what hurts so much. Exhaustive celebration in and through our suffering, which is neither distant nor sutured," is our motivation, our expression, our communication in the Clearing.[99] The beyond shouldn't be romanticized. It is terribly beautiful.[100]

We know what happens next. But Baby Suggs's sermon is sacred. So, all who have ears to hear:

> Here, in this here place, we flesh; flesh that weeps, laughs; flesh that dances on bare feet in grass. Love it. Love it hard. Yonder they do not love your flesh they despise it. They don't love your eyes; they'd just as soon pick em out. No more do they love the skin on your back. Yonder they flay it. And O my people they do not love your hands. Those they only use, tie, bind, chop off and leave empty. Love your hands! Love them. Raise them up and kiss them. Touch others with them, pat them together, stroke them on your face 'cause they don't love that either. *You* got to love it, *you!*[101]

In the Clearing, the community announced themselves as flesh through movement, through gesture. Proper language was unnecessary. In fact, proper language would have gotten in the way of their collective release.

Like "What I do," "we flesh" leaves out a verb; it does not adhere to grammar. "We flesh" cannot be hailed. It is not the production of a singular conscious subject. It leaves the relation between the collective subjectivity—the *we*—and the flesh open. Flesh could be noun or verb, substantive or active. "We flesh" might mean "*we* flesh," as in we share the same makeup, as in our sociality is our subjectivity.[102] Or it might mean "we *flesh*," as in we flesh out, as in we are those who take flesh, who express ourselves as flesh through weeping, laughing, and dancing. All of it is possible, and all of it occurs. In the Clearing, grammar doesn't matter; Baby Suggs didn't hail them—she called them.

And she didn't call them individually. They came as social, as interwoven in and through one another. They did get mixed up, after all. "Women stopped crying and danced," Morrison writes. "Men sat down and cried; children danced, women laughed, children cried until, exhausted and riven, all and each lay about the Clearing damp and gasping for breath."[103] In lieu of proper speech, crying and laughter were enough. They touched. They moved. And through these modes of engagement, they communicated. Not as mere individuals, but as flesh. Social, moving, touching flesh.

Linguist Robbins Burling tells us that there are modes of communication beyond linguistic articulation. One such mode is the analog system. Unbounded by distinction, analog systems of communication operate along a gradient. They blur together. They fail to draw sharp lines from one movement to the next.

Most of our signals, other than language, are graded [analog] rather than discrete. A giggle is not sharply distinct from a laugh, nor is a laugh clearly distinct from a guffaw. Perhaps giggles even grade into snorts, snorts into cries of objection, cries of objection into cries of anguish, and cries of anguish into sobs. . . . This is grading with a vengeance, with no boundaries in sight. The continuum may not reach quite all the way from a laugh to a sob, but human gesture-calls do show extensive grading, and this makes them utterly different from language. A halfway point between two words like *single* and *shingle* simply does not exist. A halfway point between a giggle and a laugh is perfectly real and perfectly understandable.[104]

Laughs may not always reach to a sob, but they did in the Clearing. Laughter turned into tears and then into dance, indeterminately flowing from one to the next in service of forming the possibility of social coherence. Because "there is no principled way . . . to draw a line between the end of one [gesture] and the beginning of the next," the community in the Clearing dynamically communicated along a gradient that offered the possibility of something else.[105] *I could hear him moaning and groaning.*

But the movement in the Clearing had no telos; the movement wasn't utilitarian. There was no arc that would terminate the movement; dancing turned into crying into laughter. Analog communication—grunting and gesturing—is a form of movement that cannot be hermeneutically pinned down; one cannot determine where it begins and ends. In the beyond, indeterminate movement is not an invitation to capture. It isn't denigrated; it is revered. It is primary. Indeterminate movement is the expression of fleshy release, the manifestation of flesh's freedom.

The Clearing is not simply a space of purely joyous celebration. But, analog and freed from the intention, purpose, and thinking that would announce the subject, "mixing up" was the community's mode of engagement. It was a freedom in and through—which is to say, beyond—the constraints of thought, a form of movement that could indeed bring violence but would nevertheless be uninterpretable. And mixing up prepared the community for what was to come. It wasn't until the community was "exhausted and riven" and "gasping for breath" that Baby Suggs began to preach. Crawley tells us that "exhaustion is important," that exhaustion is the condition for recovery, for speaking back "against the degradation of the flesh."[106]

This is precisely what Baby Suggs did. In the Clearing, beyond the violence of the world, Baby Suggs announced flesh's palpability, its presence.

In the beyond, we are able to see and hear flesh's call. Black flesh calls us to (and from) the beyond. The beyond makes flesh primary. The beyond allows us to see freedom in Sterling's grunts. It allows us to resonate with the freedom of Sterling's movement. It allows us to leave Sterling's speech alone, to hear it as the experimentation that it was.

Beyond takes us to a place where movement happens, but it need not be pinned down by interpretation. The beyond invites us to sit with flesh, to hear flesh's call. The beyond offers us the possibility to sit with that which cannot be categorized, holding space for that which exceeds our understanding. After Sterling was killed, Clearings erupted to show their love for Sterling's flesh. Sterling called people close. Flesh calls us close. *Let them come.*

* * *

Ieshia Evans was one of those people. "Alton Sterling's . . . killing in Baton Rouge drew me to Louisiana," she wrote.[107] Drawn to Louisiana, Evans was called—beyond herself, beyond her own possessions, beyond the constraints of the liberal subject surrounded, encumbered—possessed, as Fred Moten might say—by its own possessions.[108] "When Ferguson, Baltimore and other protests broke out," Evans claims, "I would make selfish excuses. I couldn't travel. I had to work in my job as a nurse, because I had to pay the bills. . . . This time, enough was enough. I had to do something."[109] Drawn to Baton Rouge by Sterling's flesh, Ieshia Evans responded in kind—as flesh. The Associated Press captured it on camera; the image presents her as standing, saying nothing, as cops came with their zip ties.

She, like Sterling, didn't speak. She said no words. She may not have grunted, but she stood. Silently. And standing wasn't the absence of movement. It wasn't stillness; it was stasis.[110] Tina Campt claims describes *stasis* as "unvisible motion held in tense suspension or temporary equilibrium; e.g., vibration.[111] Instead of being the absence of movement, stasis articulates a form of "black self-fashioning," steeped in tension and suspension, that offers possibility right in the middle of subjugating violence. Drawing from Darrieck Scott, Campt elaborates:

> For Scott, muscular tension represents the paradoxical power of the black body in subjection, for, as he contends, "even within the lived experience of subjugation perceived to be at its worst, there are potential powers in blackness, uses that undermine or act against racist domination." Scott's reading illuminates the forms of possibility found in the "meager resources and the failed and even

abortive strategies that flow from them because even in meagerness and failure they are rich, and not without effective capability."[112]

Campt takes Scott's work further, asking, "What if . . . we direct our attention to the affects of these women's looks?"[113] We might see something similar operative in Evans's image. She stood there, face serious, with her dress flowing in the wind. The wind was blowing; she stood against it, unwavering in her stance. We cannot see it, but her muscles had to be tensed. She stood against the wind, and against the officers. Her stance was one of the various "visible manifestations of psychic and physical *responses* (rather than submission)" to the violence of normative subjecthood.[114] Evans didn't simply stand; she stood *in the street*, gesturing toward the freedom she is and the freedom Sterling was. Flesh vibrates, even in its stasis. And as flesh, Evans stood in the Clearing opened up by Sterling's flesh. She stood in the beyond. And in standing, she announced that Sterling speaks to us from beyond.

Like Sterling's, we cannot read Evans's intentions. Like Sterling's, the meaning of Evans's movements eludes interpretive capture. Her silence and stasis leave those possibilities up to (violent) conjecture. And this is precisely what others did. Some immediately assumed that her stand was a gesture of "peaceful" protest. But Evans states otherwise. "People saw me and kept championing the 'peaceful protest,' and that's fine. . . . I'm not against protesting peacefully, and I'm not pro-violence, but I'm definitely in favor of defending yourself. When people hear the way I speak, they're usually like, 'uhh, this is not what I thought. We thought you were just about peace and holding hands!'"[115] Evans's movement was indeterminate. By standing silently, she literally gave no indication of the meaning or motivation behind her presence. But even here, the violence of enclosure visited her; people were turned off. They wanted a legible body of peaceful protest; they needed Evans to affirm the national project, and when she didn't, she was no longer the heroine. She was understood as something else. *This is grading with a vengeance, with no boundaries in sight.*

Evans shows us that Sterling's flesh doesn't invoke him alone. Taking flesh is a social move. Seeing and hearing flesh emphasizes its sociality. In the beyond, people do not announce themselves as singular, atomistic, and bounded subjects. We don't lose sight of Sterling; he remains with us. But what he communicates takes us to all those whom Sterling touched. Listening to Sterling's flesh, we cannot help but hear Cameron Sterling's cries and Quintilla McMillon's shaky voice; though we can see and hear the violence of physical oppression, we also cannot help but feel groundlife shudder under marching feet.

We've seen that contact conditions violence. The officers were "belly to belly" with Sterling when they killed him. But if contact conditions violence, it also conditions care. Proximity is as loving as it is lethal. Baby Suggs called her community to her. They began at a distance. But she called them, as flesh, from the trees. She drew them in; proximity was the conduit for release. I'm staying with love and care because this is where black flesh begins. In, through, and beyond (the violence of) the world, flesh is there, giving and receiving love through proximity. Flesh is primary—which means proximity is primary. *There is much to be praised in this / house of lightning & dust.*

Sterling and Evans both speak to fleshy indeterminacy, a fleshy *more* that resists constraint at the hands of external gazes. This more may not be enough to contradict or counteract the violence of thinking. But this more indicates that there is something beyond this violence—even as it invites such violence. This more that is flesh, this movement that announces flesh as an alternate way of being, tells us that possibility remains. Flesh remains. This remainder is critical to its constitution. And, more than this, flesh's capacities to remain name its normative thrust; flesh desires harmonious relation. Flesh demands love.

Sterling's movement was the enactment of a kind of subjectivity marked by "'loved' flesh endeavoring to make itself visible."[116] This movement, this endeavor, certainly invited death; but this death could never fully capture the excessive indeterminacy that occasioned it; although Sterling died, we will never be able to understand or entrap the meaning of Sterling's movements. And this irreducible indeterminacy, this elusive movement of black flesh, entails a freedom beyond constraint, a form of engagement beyond the categories, already worked over, with which we continue to think. Hearing and seeing Sterling, and hearing and seeing Evans, we catch glimpses of flesh—the flesh that we are, the flesh that we cannot help but be.

When we catch those glimpses, we are called to do more than think and pray.

We are called to more than emotional catharsis.

We are called to more than apology.

We are called to respond—not with violence, but with care.

In short, we are called to love.

Love it. Hard.

"I AM IRRITATED,
I REALLY AM"
BLACKNESS AS
AFFECTIVE MATTER

23.

The masses say in the streets *abolish abolish abolish*. They say Black Lives Matter against the panicked seams of a globelong eventide coming apart. Everywhere, everywhere around, something blossoms.—Canisia Lubrin, "53 Acts of Living"

There were twenty-nine of them. Some of them were short, lasting less than a minute. Others were a bit longer, going for as long as six or seven minutes. She called them "Sandy Speaks" videos, and they weren't planned; they could happen anywhere, anytime. She might be in her car or in a mall, at a museum or in her living room. Three could happen in a day.[1] She told us about issues. She told us about herself. And she reminded her viewers that they were beautiful.[2] Her reminders were her way of loving those whom she may not have seen. She loved us. She invited us to love ourselves. Her love was a gift. "I do want to let you know that there is somebody out there who loves you and who is praying for you," she once said.[3] Sandra Bland loved. She loved hard.

Sandra Bland knew of love's power. Love empowered her; she spoke powerfully. Which is to say, she spoke her mind.

> White people: Yes, black people know that all lives matter. But what I need you guys to understand is that being a black person in America is very, very hard. Although you all love to say, "Oh, nobody should see race; people are the reason racism is still alive," well, what kind of people are the reason? Black racists have no power, whereas white racists do. They have power because they are in positions of control, or they're in positions where they can influence the control over black people. Yes, that is very true. So, to my friends that want to get on my videos, and they're upset about the picture that I posted—oh well. I will not apologize for it. Because at the moment, Black. Lives. Matter. They matter.[4]

Bland loved black people. Her videos consistently ended with her saying, "Love y'all." Bland's love moved her to do things, to act. She participated in fundraisers and petitions; she highlighted black historical sites.

But her love was a complicated and problematic love. It was heterosexist. Sometimes, it was outright queerphobic. This was a love that could hurt as much as it could heal; this was a love that could be difficult to live into. We cannot overlook the complicated nature of Bland's love; it had its limits. And to overlook these limits would, itself, be unloving.

While Bland's love had its limits, her community's love for her did not. If Sandra Bland loved hard, then Rhys Caraway, a blackqueer man from Houston, loved Bland hard. When he heard the news of her death, he decided to sit vigil for her in front of the jail where she died. For at least a month, day in and day out, Rhys would make the hour-long trek from Houston to Waller County to sit vigil for a woman he never met, and who would have cringed at his queerness. (But perhaps what Rhys and others show us is that blackness and queerness cannot be disentangled. Perhaps—despite many attempts to show and prove otherwise—blackness and queerness interanimate one another.[5])

Chances are, you do not know Rhys's name. And if you don't know his name, you also probably don't know Karisha Shaw's name, either. Or Carie Cauley, Andrea Sawyer-Gray, or Secunda Joseph. The names Brandi Holmes, Malik and Jinaki Muhammad, Jessica Davenport, Stevens Orozco, Lanecia Rouse-Tinsley, Cleve Tinsley, and Chap Edmonson don't register to you. And yet, they were there. They, like Rhys, stood and sat, day in and day out, in front of that jail in hundred-degree heat to bring awareness to a woman they never met. They showed up for a woman they did not know, to whom they had no familial connection. And some of them, like Rhys, were queer, too; some of them might have been the object of Bland's disdain. But they were there. They stayed there. And beyond them, there are still others, whose names would fill pages; I do not remember them all. But I do remember that hundreds showed up. Out of love. Out of love for her.

I know these names because I was there with them. I sat in awe of their organizing brilliance; I worked with them on various projects. Chances are, you don't know these names. But that's not the point. This isn't about credit. It isn't simply about recognition. As has often been the case in black resistance movements, many of the people on the ground are overshadowed by the national names. And as is also the case, blackqueer people were at the center of this movement to raise awareness about Bland's death.[6] They didn't do it for credit. They did it because they loved her. This love exceeded the violence of this world. It exceeded the limitations of Bland's love. And for some of us, that love is queer—which is to say, that love queers the love Bland had for us.

* * *

Love is, or at least can be, a lot of things. It can be a noun: it might be a feeling or a mode of relation. It can also be a verb: love feels, and it relates. But no matter where you place it grammatically, love is capacious. It is generative. It opens worlds of possibilities. Love is powerful. Love is a power. Love empowers.

This chapter is, in part, about love. I want to sit in the space of a powerful love, a love that is so intense that it exceeds the limitations, and even the violence, of one's beloved. Audre Lorde had a word for this kind of love. She called it "eros, the personification of love in all its aspects."[7] This chapter, then, is, in part, about eros.

Bland's love may not have been Lorde's erotic. Nevertheless, it shared some resonances. Bland's love empowered her to engage with others—publicly. It inspired her to vulnerably share her feelings; it motivated her to act and to enact care.

While Bland's love may not have been (Lorde's) eros, the community's love for Bland was. In Bland, we catch a glimpse of Lorde's eros, but in the Clearing that formed in Bland's wake, we are engulfed by it. ("*Wake: a watch or vigil held beside the body of someone who has died, sometimes accompanied by ritual observances including eating and drinking.*")[8] In Bland, we are able see the depth, creativity, integrity, and power of sharing feelings, but in the Clearing enacted in Bland's wake, we are able to see how far this power can stretch. Maybe seeing these things enraptures us; perhaps they empower us to love—Bland and others.

This chapter is also, in part, about pornography. If love, erotic love, is about feeling, then Lorde has another term with which we must wrestle: *the pornographic*. For Lorde, pornography uses and abuses feeling.[9] It instrumentalizes it. Pornography is solely self-gratifying. It's voyeuristic. And for this reason, pornography is the affective register for the subject. Brian Encinia stopped Bland on the side of the road. During this stop, he suggested that Bland was irritated. She confirmed that she was. And this irritation moved him. It unsettled him. It compelled him to pull her out of the car and violently manhandle her.

As is the case with each of these stories, Encinia was compelled to do so. Through his actions to and upon Bland, Encinia established himself as a public servant. Drawing from her expression of irritation, Encinia outed himself as a subject who could not help but establish itself through violence against a black body—a black female body. Subjects form and are formed through their pornographic use of blackness, of black flesh; this is a form of use that cannot help but abuse. Subjects love pornography. They love to gaze. And it was precisely Encinia's inability to gaze—to constitute, to make sense of Bland—that moved him.

These two registers—the erotic and the pornographic—name, respectively, the felt and affective underpinnings of religious experience. They name the feeling sociality that is flesh, and they also name the pornographic violence that both produces and manipulates bodies. Eros and pornography aren't divested of power relations; the (post)phenomenology of religious experience they motivate isn't disentangled from the structures of this world. In fact, it is infused with them.[10] For this reason, I, too, will infuse the erotic section and the pornographic section of this chapter with meditations on religious experience.

On the one hand, eros is spiritual. Ashon Crawley's black pneuma comes to mind here; it is the breath that holds us together, that provides the life in the midst of ever-present death. Flesh breathes. And such breathing is the capacity for generative connection, for a different kind of sociality. Flesh only has, it only *is*, sociality. Erotic sociality. Shared feelings. Shared feeling. "*We* flesh," Baby Suggs preaches. And that *we* matters.

But Baby Suggs was no fool. She also knew about the yonder. "Yonder they do not love your flesh." The yonder is where pornography reigns. The yonder is the world of the subject, where black flesh is "slopped for hogs." This slopping is compulsory. It occurs because black flesh *moves* subjects. In the yonder, black flesh is the subject's unmoved mover.

This movement isn't a logical relation, though. It is a phenomenological one. And it is affective. The subject is unsettled—irritated—by black flesh. It cannot turn away, but it cannot *not* turn away. Encinia pursued Bland. She allured him. But she also concerned him. She became an object of simultaneous concern and attraction. After he stopped her, he lingered. He couldn't leave. He couldn't simply give the warning. Black flesh is alluring and terrifying for the subject. The experience exceeds reason. It is religious. In the presence of black flesh, the subject finds its object of religious experience.

Do not think of the "twoness" in this chapter as a binary logic. The Clearing and the yonder invoke one another. Though we hope for the dissolution of the yonder, it nevertheless is present; flesh makes bodies possible. Bodies, in turn, invoke flesh's excessive unruliness. Bland was situated between the two registers. She lived as both. Her life and death remind us of blackness's excessive presence in this world. In the yonder, Encinia pornotroped Bland into a pornographic object for his own enjoyment; she died three days later. But in the Clearing, she was posthumously caressed by erotic love. Black, fleshy, erotic love. Bland was both. Blackness is both.

We must attend to both. And we begin with eros.

Love, Feeling, Flesh: Erotic Feeling as Flesh's Mode of Engagement and Expression

"Love y'all" was Bland's constant refrain. In each of the "Sandy Speaks" videos, Bland consistently told her viewers that she loved them. This love appears as commitment. It shows up as a decision not to turn away from those for whom Bland cared.

Bland especially loved children. The first video she uploaded made her purpose clear: these videos were "for the children." Perhaps this commitment to children stemmed from the fact that she had lost her own unborn child. In her jail intake interview (can we call that an interview?), Bland disclosed that she'd had a miscarriage, and that this miscarriage brought a severe amount of mental anguish: she'd attempted to kill herself.[11] Though the attempt wasn't successful, it appears to have left an indelible mark on her consciousness.

Sandy's love for children, then, came from a place of pain. But it also produced her commitment. For example, she consistently engaged with the Jackie Robinson West Little League baseball team. The team had won the world championship, but, due to a technicality, the league stripped them of their title. The team didn't intentionally gain an upper hand; there were no funny financial dealings, no manipulated equipment. There were no cork bats. The boys were all of the right age, and they were all of the right size. It just so happened that some of the boys didn't live in the district where the team was located.

Perhaps this was the case because there weren't other teams where some of these boys lived. Perhaps, unlike their subject counterparts, these kids didn't have the mobility to pack up and move to a place for better opportunities. It didn't matter. Some coach from another team couldn't abide losing (perhaps to black kids), and it came to light that all the boys didn't come from the same place. The championship was expunged.[12]

Bland wanted to reinstate the championship. She wanted those boys to retain the reward for the work they'd put in. Armed with a stack of petitions, she went to malls and coffee shops to get signatures to get the championship reinstated. She did this on her own time and her own dime. She was committed. And she was committed because she loved.

Bland's love was complicated, though. *Complicated* is actually an understatement: Bland's commitment to black communities came with an expressed heterosexist lens. "Being gay is a choice," she once said. "Being black ain't."[13] In remembering Sandra Bland, we can't forget this. Her love for black communities primarily included black cisgendered heterosexual people. Her in/capacity to tolerate, let alone embrace, blackqueerness demonstrates that Bland's love had its limitations.

There is another form of love, however, that is capacious. It exceeds the limitations of Bland's love. It enacts love for Bland despite her own limits. Audre Lorde called this kind of love "erotic." Lorde spoke of eros because she knew that it is a portal to possibility. It is a portal to creativity. Erotic love names the capacity to share and to build together, and it is steeped in queerness, in the capacity of blackqueer people—particularly blackqueer women—to live, care, create, and build with one another. I turn to Lorde as an homage to those blackqueer people who, for some time now, have often been at the forefront of organizing efforts. Their love is erotic. It will care even for those who do not care for them. Erotic love moves beyond the heteronormative constrictions of this world. It enacts a care that exceeds the violence of this world, even when that violence is directed toward those of us who are queer.

Erotic love is affective. It is (about) feeling. "The erotic," Lorde wrote, "is a measure between the beginnings of our sense of self and the chaos of our strongest feelings. It is an internal sense of satisfaction to which, once we have experienced it, we know we can aspire."[14] Eros is situated between selfhood and feelings; it ties the two together, such that "selfhood," whatever this term may come to designate, cannot be fully satisfied without entangling itself with feelings—chaotic, undirected feelings. This isn't quite the "Affect" of many approaches to affect studies. And it is so much more than Affect.[15]

What we now call *affect theory* wasn't quite a thing when Lorde wrote. Maybe this is why much of affect studies still doesn't turn to her—even though much of affect theory's genealogy goes back before Lorde's time.[16] But Lorde's work is steeped in affect; she understood the constructive capacities of anger; she hated the "plasticized sensation" of pornographic affect (more on that later).[17] For Lorde, "affect" shapes the world of the ascetic, "who aspires to feel nothing" (more on this later, too).[18] So, although she spoke of affect, her erotic lens pushed her to prefer feelings. Eros sits with feelings. It sits with feeling. Grammatically, the term *feeling* can be a noun or a gerund: you can have a feeling, or you might exist as feeling—joy, sadness, anger, or perhaps even rage. Because of its grammatical plasticity, *feeling* doesn't need a grammatical subject. On the gerund side, it's already built in. Subjects can (try to) attach themselves to it, but such attachment is unnecessary. To sit with feeling—particularly shared feeling—then, is to sit in a space beyond the world of the subject. It is to move and exist in and as relation.

Lorde turned to feeling as a way to speak of fullness, of depth. Eros is feeling; love is feeling. But it is also the quality of feeling, the contours of feeling, the fullness that feeling can provide. "The erotic," she wrote, "is not a question only of what we do; it is a question of how acutely and fully we can feel in the doing."[19] Erotic feeling is about fullness.

Erotic love is also sensual, and it is about the constructive power of such sensuality. Sensuality—which includes, but exceeds, sensation; Lorde's eros is always and already shared, and it is shared because it is sensual, because it moves between, in, and as flesh.

To sit with erotic feeling, then, is to sit with flesh. Flesh is nothing and everything. As I discussed in chapter 2, Spillers and Merleau-Ponty announce flesh's ontological and sociopolitical antecedence to the subject and its phenomenological perspective. Flesh is both body parts and the sinews that hold body parts together. It is the capacity to touch as well as the touch itself; flesh feels and enables feeling. Flesh and feeling fold over and into one another.

Flesh, black flesh, then, is erotic. It touches and makes touch possible. It touches and is touched. And it yearns for these touches to be loving touches.[20] Such touches dissolve the very capacity for subject formation. To touch and be touched is to lose mastery, to lose one's centrality to the primacy of caring relation. It is to lose, and, subsequently, to no longer desire, primacy. Touching is an abdication of subjective primacy.

Eros, then, must be shared; it cannot be the sole property of one individual. "The sharing of joy, whether physical, emotional, psychic, or intellectual, forms a bridge between the sharers which can be the basis for understanding much of what is not shared between them, and lessens the threat of their difference."[21]

It is sourced from a subjective dissolution, from a formation that is a deformation, through touch. Toni Morrison knew about touch's dehiscent capacities. In chapter 2, I turned to the Clearing in *Beloved* to announce the beyond where flesh resides, the place where flesh yearns and receives love and care. But there are other places where flesh speaks in the novel, places where flesh's existence as condition and manifestation shows itself. If flesh speaks unintelligibly and moves indeterminately, then Beloved, Sethe's killed daughter, also and always speaks as flesh. She is simply relation—violent, passionate, loving relation: she drew Denver closer to her; she (parasitically) connected with Sethe; and she had sex with Paul D, breaking open the cold tin container in his heart in order for him to feel (again). Beloved's love was erotic—even, perhaps in its violence.[22]

Beloved's love was also fleshy: she spoke indeterminately.

it is always now there will never be a time when I am not crouching and watching others who are crouching too I am always crouching the man on my face is dead his face is not mine his mouth smells sweet but his eyes are locked
    some who eat nasty themselves I do not eat the men without skin bring us their morning water to drink we have none at night I cannot see the dead man on my face daylight comes through the cracks and I can see his locked eyes I am not big small rats do not wait for us to sleep someone is thrashing but there is no room to do it in if we had more to drink we could make tears we cannot make sweat or morning water so the men without skin bring us theirs one time they bring us sweet rocks to suck we are all trying to leave our bodies

behind the man on my face has done it it is hard to make yourself die forever you sleep short and then return in the beginning we could vomit now we do not . . .

the woman is there with the face I want the face that is mine . . . if I had the teeth of the man who died on my face I would bite the circle around her neck bite it away I know she does not like it [23]

Beloved is "trying to leave her body behind," which can be read as both physical and ontological death. She is trying to leave behind her body to physically die, yes; she is also leaving her body behind to move beyond the embodied boundaries of the subject. This passage, then, can be read as yearning for relation, to be in relation, to *be* relation. After all, it is only *after* Beloved expresses her desire to leave her body that she yearns to liberate the woman who has the "face that is mine." Beloved's face is also the face of the other. Beloved isn't a subject. She is flesh. She speaks as flesh. And she moves as flesh.

Beloved also feels as flesh. She senses the "morning water"; she smells the sweetness of the man's mouth. She also has desire. She desires to free another. And she does so because she loves the woman—to the point where the woman is her: "I am not separate from her there is no place where I stop her face is my own and I want to be there in the place where her face is and to be looking at it too."[24] Beloved feels. And she loves. Her love is her feeling—and I use the term *feeling* as gerund here: love is Beloved's way of feeling. And she does so as flesh. Beloved is flesh. She speaks as flesh. She moves as flesh. And she feels as flesh. Feeling is flesh's mode of engagement.

Feeling has depth. And it has expansiveness. As gerund, feeling is a mode of engagement. It is a capacity that exceeds the specific person. Feeling, erotic feeling, doesn't need an object; it only needs to *be*. Like hands touching one another, erotic feeling just . . . is. Left alone, erotic feeling is a quality that infuses the whole of experience with its fullness. Like a yellow pellet applied to colorless margarine, eros fills experience with depth and satisfaction.[25] Feeling, erotic feeling—which is to say, erotic love—needs no project. It does its work freely. It satisfies.

But this satisfaction is shared. The erotic doesn't stay contained within a bounded subject. In fact, as Amber Jamilla Musser, reflecting on Audre Lorde, writes, "the route to subjecthood is community."[26] Erotic love flows through and beyond us. It motivates us to "live from within outward," ultimately "illuminating our actions upon the world around us."[27] As the depths of feeling, erotic love transcends us through its immanent fullness. It overtakes us. We are overwhelmed by it. Once we're touched by it, we yearn for it. We can't get enough of it.[28]

> Many days I long for you wanting you
> Hoping for the chance to get to know you
> Longing for your kiss
> For your touch
> Your feel
> Your essence (yeah)
> Many nights I've cried from the things you do
> Felt like I could die from the thought of losing you
> I know that you're real
> With no doubts
> No fears
> And no questions.[29]

We fall in/to love. Erotic love grips us. It holds us. Musiq Soulchild's song "Love" announces love's capacity to dissolve our self-preoccupation in favor of another—of an-Other. Erotic love preoccupies our thoughts and colors our perceptions. Having fallen in/to love, we struggle to speak intelligibly, preferring to touch, to feel, to caress.[30] Having abandoned the capacity to speak in*tell*igibly, erotic love prompts our turn to the sensual— which exceeds the sensible.[31] Eros exceeds the sensibility of the subject by (being) feeling. As feeling, eros transcends through immanence.

Eros as Religious Experience

Baby Suggs was a preacher. "Love it hard" is a homiletic proclamation. The relationship between love and religious experience is a close one. Perhaps love, eros, is its own form of religious experience.

Lorde knew this. She claimed that erotic feeling is spiritual, and she refused to distinguish the spiritual from the political.[32] Baby Suggs also knew this: "She told them that the only grace they could have was the grace they could imagine. That if they could not see it, they would not have it."[33] These women understood love's power. They allowed it to fill their lives. And in so doing, they allowed it to permeate their actions. Love motivated them—to write and act, to call, and, yes, to share this love through videos and collective action. And, perhaps, such actions were sourced from the depths of feeling, from the fullness of an experience that could not help but motivate one to speak, to act, and to act out. "Recognizing the power of the erotic within our lives," Lorde writes, "can give us the energy to pursue genuine change within our world, rather than merely settling for a shift of characters in the same weary drama."[34] Perhaps feeling, erotic feeling, with its spiritual roots, is precisely the capacity to critique the violence of this world *through* religious experience. Which is to say, perhaps erotic feeling, as spiritual, *is* religious experience.

Spiritual is a tricky term. It often conjures up new religious movements and dialectical philosophies. Hegel used it to turn consciousness into a logical problem. But there are other appropriations of spirit. Lorde gave us one; Ashon Crawley gave us another. They resonate with one another; they are about sharing. For Lorde, it was sharing feelings. For Crawley, it is the sharing of breath.

For Crawley, black breath, "black *pneuma*," is an invitation to possibility. It is life. It is a form of life done differently. It names the capacity for life right in the midst of overwhelming restriction. Flesh doesn't simply breathe, though. (Often, it can't.) As the threat of suffocation looms, flesh breathes differently. It breathes *like that*.[35] It breathes *otherwise*.[36] The *otherwise* isn't set in opposition—or even apposition—to the sedimented intellectual traditions that wrestle only with bodies and subjects; instead, it stands as a prior resistance to constriction, a freedom that cannot remain unchecked. Flesh's breath, flesh's spirit, conditions thought even as it eludes thought.[37] Flesh breathes in relation. It breathes as relation. To breathe—and especially to breathe *like that*—is to already indicate that one's existence is already social. It's already excessive. It doesn't comprehend; it need not do so.

To breathe, then, even as the trees do, is to already invite excess.[38] Breathing in, I breathe in my environment—which means I breathe in the excess of others. I've already rendered myself porous through the act of inhalation; I've already invited others to penetrate me when I inhale.

Breathing out, I contribute to—or detract from—the environment, which means I am already connected to others. Breathing is a form of transcendence into the social. Breathing reminds us of the flesh that we always and already are. Indeed, as Levinas writes, the otherwise than being—the "beyond essence" of ethical relation—is already an excess, but an excess in reverse, as one is rendered passive "beyond all passivity" in the face of the other.[39] In and as the beyond of the subject, black flesh breathes a different kind of life. Breath is relation. Breath is shared. Breathing is an act of sharing. It is erotic.

Lorde and Crawley remind us that eros is spiritual. It is an invitation. It prompts us to share and be shared. It releases us from the constrictive violence of this world. Flesh may be reduced to bodies, but when it breathes—which it always does—it exceeds this violence. And, in breathing—in laughing, dancing, and crying—flesh connects. It forms sociality. It *is* sociality. It forms love. It *is* love. It is transcendence into the sociality it always and already is. *I* becomes *we*, as in *We flesh*.

What I am trying to say here is that the spirituality to which Lorde and Crawley attune us is a modality of religious experience. To laugh, dance, and cry for the living and the dead is to enact what Anthony Pinn might call the quest for complex subjectivity; it is the flesh's enactment of life in the midst of the yonder, in the midst of what Pinn calls "historical objectification."[40] Pinn will tell us that this quest is steeped in making sense of our lives; he'll claim that religious experience "is . . . presented as a 'feeling' that informs or substantiates our wrestling with history."[41] If our bodies are to be slopped for hogs, then the feeling to which Pinn points is a yearning for black flesh to be loved, to be held and remembered even as it is visited by violence, by the violence of history and the ongoing violence of the present.

Riffing off Pinn, I would suggest that Lorde's erotic and Crawley's breath disclose this feeling as always and already steeped in sociality, in relation, in and through the bonds we forge and try to maintain. The Clearing is a religious space not simply because of the liturgical structure of its unfolding, but also because it invites the working out of—not simply the reflection on—the meaning of our existence. "We flesh" is a prayer. The Clearing is a space of religious experience. Told you Baby Suggs was a preacher.

Perhaps this is why so many people showed up for Bland after she died. In the wake of her death, black people, blackqueer people, raised awareness about her, about the brutality enacted against her. This community of black people, this mass of black flesh, showed itself in love and care for Bland's flesh. And in so doing, they expressed Lorde's erotic; they articulated a kind of transcendence into the social, a modality of existence that never leaves this world but nevertheless yearns for otherwise possibilities right here and right now. They sat vigil. They prayed. They laughed. They danced. They cried—for the dead. Which is to say, they *breathed*. They breathed *like that*. They breathed *otherwise*.

I know they did this.

Because I was there. Laughing, dancing, and crying right along with them.

Pornography: Flattening Feeling into Affect

Brian Encinia wasn't there with us.[42] He'd already shown himself. He was, in part, how we got to know—and somehow never knew—Sandy. He'd met her three days before she died. And when he did, he was on edge.

> INTERVIEWER: Explain for the recording why you decided to make a driver's-side approach.
>
> ENCINIA: . . . I'd already observed Ms. Bland making numerous furtive movements, including disappearing from view for an amount of time. I walked back to the driver's side because it allowed me a better angle through the untinted windows to view the driver and any possible actions or movements I'd already witnessed. That's why I made a driver's-side approach, because I could see her better, as far as officer safety. . . .
>
> INTERVIEWER: Explain for the recording why you would go from . . . a routine traffic stop with an aggravated person that in your opinion . . . she's agitated, to your thought process that, there's a possibility that you need to make a driver's-side approach due to your training on officers being shot.
>
> ENCINIA: . . . Because, when I was still inside the patrol car, I'd seen numerous movements, to the right, to the console, her right side of her body, that area, as well as disappearing from sight. That being said, through my training experience, it's possible that a weapon and/or drugs could be, uh, stuffed away or retrieved, making that . . . driver's-side approach, she had untinted glass on her windows, so I would be able to see . . . if anything would possibly be in her hands, if she had to turn over her shoulder or not. Um, so that's why.[43]

Encinia is recounting his encounter with Sandra Bland on July 10, 2015. That day would be the last day of Bland's freedom; he would arrest her on the side of the road for "assault on a public servant." Bland would die in jail three days later.

Some might be wondering why the "driver's-side approach" is central to this line of questioning. If you've seen the video, then you know it begins with Encinia approaching Bland from the passenger side, but, after he writes the warning, he approaches the driver's side. Encinia claims that, according to his training, passenger-side approaches put the officer in more danger; the driver has more room to move, and therefore—again, according to Encinia's training—could injure or maim the officer. He makes a driver's-side approach, then, because he was concerned for his safety.

Safety is an interesting term, though. What triggered his concern for his safety? Was it really just her movement? That's possible (see chapter 2). And—*and*—it also seems that he was already concerned for his safety before the stop. Brian Collister takes the story from here:

> Encinia said Bland had driven through a stop sign as she left the Prairie View A&M campus, but the trooper admitted he was unsure if it was on private or public property. "I was unsure at the time if that stop sign was located at a public or private roadway," said Encinia.
>
> Knowing he could not ticket Bland for failure to stop at the sign, Encinia went on to explain why he followed her. "I was checking the condition of the vehicle, such as the make, the model, had a license plate, any other conditions."[44]

Encinia followed her. He tailed her. He stopped her. Bland was minding her own business. She wasn't concerned with or about Encinia. But he was concerned with and about her.

Let Encinia tell it though, he was concerned *for* her. As he stops her, Encinia walks to the window. He gives his reason for the traffic stop. And then, he immediately asks her, "What's wrong?" We cannot see Bland in this moment; the dashcam video doesn't show her expressions. But there is a palpable exasperation in her voice as she responds to Encinia's questions. A dialogue ensues.

ENCINIA: You okay?

BLAND: I'm waiting on you—this is your job. I'm waiting on you [inaudible]—

ENCINIA: I don't know—you seem very irritated.

BLAND: I am, I really am, 'cause I feel like it's crap with what I'm getting a ticket for. I was getting out of your way, and you were speeding up, tailing me, so I move over, and you stop me. So, yeah, I am a little irritated—but that doesn't stop you from giving me a ticket, so . . .[45]

What happens next is brutal. After a few seconds, Encinia sarcastically says, "Are you done?" Bland responds by saying, "You asked me what was wrong with me, so I told you, so yeah, I'm done." Encinia says, "Okay." But then he makes an unusual demand: "You mind putting out your cigarette please, if you don't mind." Bland doesn't comply; there's no legal statute for having to put out one's cigarette.

Physical violence ensues. Whatever concern Encinia had for Bland's condition went out the window. Encinia asks her to get out of the car. She refuses. Encinia opens the door, proceeds to pull her out of the car, and asks for backup. Encinia eventually wrestles her to the ground, amid her loud screams and protests. At one point, they move beyond the frame of the camera, and all we can hear is Bland screaming and Encinia trying to subdue her. He eventually arrests Bland for "Assault on a Public Servant," the judge sets her bail for five thousand dollars, and three days later, she is found dead, hanging in her jail cell from a trash bag.[46] "Concern" led to death.

This concern, it seems, had everything to do with Bland's affective state. She was "irritated," and, for Encinia, this irritation was more than irritation. It was also anger.

INTERVIEWER: Did she seem agitated at that time?

ENCINIA: She did not seem nervous. She seemed somewhat angry.[47]

The interviewer seems confused, so he asks other questions: Had Encinia seen people angry with him before? *Yes.* Did he always make driver's-side approaches when this happened? *No.* What was different this time? *She was moving—furtively—to her right side.* Had you seen other people move in this way? *Yes.* Did you treat them the same? *No.* The ambiguity is on full display. What was it, then, that prompted Encinia to continue to interrogate Bland? Why was he concerned for his safety?

My hunch—and I admit, it's just a hunch—is that it was Bland's affective state that kept Encinia glued to the scene.[48] After all, the interviewer asked him whether or not he saw anything illegal, any weapons—anything—that would prompt this concern.

INTERVIEWER: You said there was nothing overt—no weapons seen, nothing like that, correct?

ENCINIA: Nothing in plain view, that was correct.[49]

The question is asked multiple times. And the answer is the same. Bereft of evidence, Encinia's concern seems misplaced. Unless, of course, it was Bland's affective state that put him on edge. What Encinia appeared to want—what he appeared to need—was for Bland to be pleasant. Encinia desired that Bland be pleasant to him. He wanted her to be happy. He wanted her to be merry. And this desire is as old as antiblack chattel slavery itself.

> The brutal command to merrymaking suggest[s] that the theatricality of the Negro emerges only in the aftermath of the body's brutal dramatic displacement—in short, after the body has been made subject to the will of the master. . . . What else could jigs danced in command performances be but the gentle indices of domination[?] . . . Such performances cast the slave as contented bondsman and elide the difference between volition and violation.[50]

Hartman is clear here: white people needed to vindicate themselves by noting that enslaved black people were "content," happy—pleased—to be in and of service to those who lorded power over their bodies. Smile, or be beaten: your choice.

Encinia doesn't put the choice in such stark terms. But he clued in on her "irritation" at the scene, and, as he reflected later in his interview, her affective state concerned him.

> INTERVIEWER: You wrote in your report, "I knew . . . based on her demeanor, that something was wrong." Explain for the recording what you thought was wrong.
>
> ENCINIA: At that time, I observed, it was her body language, her actions, uh, her demeanor—it appeared that she was not okay.[51]

Bland's "body language" and "demeanor" were the culprits. It might not seem like demeanor and body language are connected to affect, but, as most affect studies folks know, affect gives you away:

> My clammy hands; the note of anger in your voice; the sparkle of glee in their eyes. You may protest your innocence, but we both know, don't we, that who you *really* are, or *what* you really are, is going to be found in the pumping of your blood, the quantity and quality of your perspiration, the breathless anticipation in your throat, the way you can't stop yourself from grinning, the glassy sheen in your eyes.[52]

Let Encinia tell it, then, Bland's body language and demeanor gave her away as one who was irritated. And this was enough for him to be concerned. This was enough for him to linger without any evidence of threat or violence. The threat was affect itself. Encinia saw nothing of concern, but—again, let him tell it—it wasn't what he was seeing, but rather what he couldn't see. "It's the unknown, what I *can't* see, is what I had a concern with," he claims in the interview. And he repeats himself: "To me, it's still the unknown."[53] Encinia couldn't see "what was wrong," but he was affected by it. Whatever this *it* was, *it* unsettled him, left him disoriented.

I might hazard that this *it* was irritation. After all, he noted that Bland seemed "irritated" when he stopped her. Perhaps Bland's irritation was what concerned Encinia. Perhaps Bland's irritation became Encinia's justification for Bland's demise. *You seem very irritated.*

I know that irritation is an ugly feeling. I know that it is ill equipped to spur constructive political possibilities. And yet, I'm also aware that "it is irritation's radical *in*adequacy . . . that calls attention to a symbolic violence in the principle of commensurability itself, when there is an underlying assumption that an appropriate emotional response to racist violence exists, and that the burden lies on the racialized subject to produce that appropriate response legibly, unambiguously, and immediately."[54] Bland's irritation was just enough—which means, it wasn't nearly enough.

Irritation's inadequacy superficializes it.[55] Bland became an affective surface when she confirmed her irritation; she was an irritant. And this, in turn, irritated Encinia. The affective encounter on July 10 entailed a pornographic relation: Encinia used Bland's feelings—her irritation—as a "Kleenex."[56]

The lack of apparent depth—the outward presence of irritation—allowed Encinia to simply read Bland as a body, as a surface. Bland's body, as a surface, was irritated; it was affective inflammation. And this inflammation, according to Encinia, erupted into "combativeness"; it resulted in injuries to his body.[57] Encinia claims that Bland became combative, that she—in her irritation—resisted his commands. Bland's irritation, then, retroactively served Encinia's purposes; it was ultimately used for his abdication. Consider Encinia's police report, quoted below:

> I had Bland exit the vehicle to further conduct a safe traffic investigation. Bland became combative and uncooperative. Numerous commands were given to Bland ordering her to exit the vehicle. Bland was removed from the car but became more combative. Bland was placed in handcuffs for officer safety. Bland began swinging her elbows at me and then kicked my right leg in the shin. I had a pain in my right leg and suffered small cuts on my right hand. Force was used to subdue Bland to the ground to which Bland continued to fight back. Bland was placed under arrest for Assault on Public Servant. . . . The vehicle was inventoried

and released to Crown Towing. Bland was transported and booked into Waller County Jail for Assault on Public Servant.[58]

At first glance, it would seem that Bland is the culprit; her combativeness became a threat to the officer's safety. Encinia claimed he had to use force on Bland for his own protection. And, in fact, it is very possible that he was afraid—that he did, indeed, fear for his safety in the presence of a black female body. Bland, after all, was honest and not submissive. She didn't hold her tongue.

It is possible, then, that Bland's assertiveness—that both challenged and irritated Encinia—also scared him. This is particularly the case with black women, as their bodies—to again return to Spillers—are supposed to exhibit "sheer physical powerlessness that slides into a more general 'powerlessness,' resonating through various centers of human and social meaning."[59] The black female body is *supposed* to be powerless, and when it isn't, when it resists, it becomes threatening. Bland was irritated, and she was assertive, which meant—affectively—that she could have done anything. Threat.[60]

Encinia's claim that "Bland was placed in handcuffs for officer safety" confirms this. This isn't the actuality of a dangerous individual; Encinia saw nothing but an "irritated" and assertive black woman. Her irritation threatened him, and so he cut the threat short by subduing it. He compromised his own safety through his use of force. He generated fear through his preemptive actions, made possible by the threat of Bland's "combativeness."

Pornographizing and Pornotroping Blackness: Affective Feedback Loops

According to Encinia, though, Bland wasn't simply irritated. In his interview, the terms *irritation, aggravation,* and *anger* become synonymous; Encinia can't keep his affects together.

This makes sense. After all, flesh expresses in an analog fashion; it mixes things up. It is very possible, then, that Bland *was* angry, that she *was* aggravated—and all of this would make sense if we understand her as flesh. What Encinia perceived—but couldn't see—was fleshy feeling at play. As the dashcam footage unfolds, Bland appears to move through multiple feelings, often at the same time. After Encinia pulls her out of the car, she begins by saying things like, "Let's do this" and "I can't wait!," registering her excitement at the possibility of suing Encinia. But as the encounter continues to unfold and Encinia increases his brutality, excitement turns to fear, which turns to anger, which turns to terror, and then they all get mixed up. Bland pleads with Encinia as he swings her; she lets him know she has epilepsy. She screams. She cries. She sobs—uncontrollably. She curses; she screams all kinds of invectives at Encinia. The affects get mixed up. The feelings get mixed up. Bland was angry, *and* she was irritated. She was also scared. She was also excited. There were no hard distinctions between anger, irritation, and aggravation because flesh doesn't split the affects out this way.[61] The mixing up is there. Flesh. Black flesh.

Hortense Spillers tells us that flesh is the capacity for one to register wounding. July 10, 2015, shows us this capacity. It shows us that, at the end of the day, flesh is both the condition of and for care as well as the capacity to register the violence of subjects, to feel the depths of this violence. Encinia's inability to keep his affects—and therefore his story—together reflects this. He perceived moving flesh; he felt living matter. And, as was the case with Weekley, Loehmann, Salamoni, and Lake, Encinia couldn't help himself. He enacted a form of brutality—perhaps just short of death—against black female flesh.

He didn't read it this way, of course. I'm not sure he *could* have read it this way. There was only one affect for Encinia: concern. Encinia was only concerned. This concern correlated to his safety. There were no other possibilities. Subjects turn what was once, and still is, analogical into single realities. Subjects reduce senses to *sense*. They do not feel; they flatten feeling into affects.[62] And then, by some twist of theoretical fate, affects become Affect.[63] Blurred and blurry feelings are gone; something is either Affect or it isn't. Either/or. On/off. Digital.[64] (Virtual?)[65]

Encinia, then, didn't feel. He was affected, but he didn't feel. He tells us as much: when the interviewer asks him if he was angered by Bland's words, he replies, "We are taught to be impartial and unbiased. I was not agitated or upset." He *was* concerned—about Bland, for his own safety, about the unknown, about what he couldn't see—but this concern was more Heideggerian than anything else.[66] "I always have safety concerns," he said. He was concerned about what was affecting *him*, about what *he* could see or not see. He was concerned for his own practical subjectivity. He was concerned—or perhaps he cared—about his identity as a public servant.[67] Bland was simply the affective site that confirmed his position, his identity, his subjectivity. It was about him. It was always about him. *I always have safety concerns.*

Perhaps concern is, also, an affect. Affects are, after all, autotelic. Though they bounce around, though they flow through and between bodies, they ultimately return to themselves.[68] In their semistable existence as structures that can be shared over time and space, they nevertheless satisfy *themselves*. They are the source of their own satisfaction; they feed back into themselves. Affects love feedback loops—maybe they *are* feedback loops. For affective and affected subjects, everything is feedback. Which is to say, everything feeds back to them—even the violence of this world.[69]

Lorde had a term for the kind of subjective engagement that relies upon autotelic and feedback-based affects: pornography.[70] For Lorde, the pornographic is "sensation without feeling." The pornographic is an "abuse of feeling" that entails "[using] each other as objects of satisfaction."[71] The satisfaction is never shared. It always comes back to the one who engages in pornography. The sensations make the subject feel better. Subjects use these sensations for their own satisfaction.

Pornography has a discursive and ontological correlate. Hortense Spillers calls it "pornotroping." It is the process of turning black female flesh into an object of "irresistible, destructive sensuality" that "embodies a physical powerlessness that slides into a more general 'powerlessness,' resonating through various centers of human and social meaning."[72] We've already seen a variant of this in chapter 1: police officers and public officials pornotroped Mertilla Jones and Samaria Rice in order to justify the violence they enacted and supported against Aiyana and Tamir. To pornotrope is to turn black flesh, black female flesh, into an object of and for the subject's desires and whims. Pornotroping is a compulsive act: black flesh, black female flesh, is irresistible. But pornotroping is a compulsive death-dealing act. The sensuality is destructive. Subjects cannot help but attempt to destroy the black flesh to which they are helplessly attracted—by which I mean, subjects cannot help but turn black flesh into black bodies, and therefore into black objects.[73] "Stripped flesh," Weheliye writes, "particularly in concurrence with brutality, represents a primary aspect of pornotroping in the beyond."[74] Pornotroping and pornography invoke one another. They are twin capacities of the subject. Pornotroping flesh into bodies, subjects flatten black fleshy feelings into racialized affects that, in turn, pornographically satisfy the subjects themselves.

If encounters like these weren't so frequent, and did not have a considerable history behind them, we might be able to disentangle Encinia's action-induced concern from Bland's blackness and femaleness. Pornographic pornotroping is not new. A white man physically overpowering a black woman and using her for his own whims has its history. It has its *histories*. These stories should not be told. They never should have happened. But they did. And they are with us.

These memories don't always rise to the level of awareness. They flow through our encounters. We remember them, but not cognitively; they—the stories and the agents—have become "incorporeal material."[75] They—the stories and the agents—have become virtual.[76] They structure the potential flows of Affect. Pornographic Affect. Subjects become subjects *through* pornographically autotelic affects. In turn, they are compelled to pornotrope—which in turn provides satisfaction for the subject. It is concerning to be concerned. And, having become concerned, one is the one for whom concern is an issue. Feedback.

PORNOGRAPHIC PORNOTROPING AS RELIGIOUS EXPERIENCE

Bland moved Encinia. He was moved by her. As stated above, Encinia followed her—for no reason, other than what appears to be concern. Bland was, indeed, minding her own business. She was driving, but she was unmoved—by him, anyway.

Encinia's pursuit requires more investigation. There was something about Bland that moved him, that animated him, that called him into being. It was affective. To be always concerned, and then to turn that concern into pursuit, and then brutality, is to be moved by another, to be affected by another. An-Other.

Encinia didn't simply follow Bland. After he stopped her, after he decided to give her a warning, he decided to linger. The interviewer asks why he stayed at the scene, and Encinia responds.

> INTERVIEWER: You wrote earlier . . . that you already knew she was agitated with you when you approached her. . . . You've seen her hands, you don't see anything overtly, and you ask her, "Are you okay?" Do you think you prolonged the traffic stop? Or should you have issued her the warning and put her on her way?
>
> ENCINIA: [*stammers*] I used the time to . . . reevaluate and check the condition of the vehicle—again, if anything had been moved, or whatnot, and I checked her [*stammers*] and again it's still me having the reasonable suspicion of that area of control.[77]

The interviewer isn't convinced. If Encinia was so concerned, so the line of thinking goes, why didn't he ask her to get out of the car then? "I was still processing everything," he says. And then, an odd statement: "It took time to view her, and her actions and her demeanor, and her body language as well as to look around her area of control. It took time." He lingered because he wanted to continue viewing her. He lingered because he needed to look—to gaze.[78] He couldn't look away.

Encinia gives no good reason why he stayed. Twenty-six seconds go by, the interviewer claims; you see nothing, smell nothing, hear nothing—all you notice is that Bland is agitated. And—*and*—you've already decided to give her a warning. Why linger? Why stay? Encinia lingers so long that it becomes unreasonable—at least to the questioner, anyway.

> INTERVIEWER: How long do you think is reasonable under ordinary circumstances to keep someone—once you've decided to issue them a warning, there's nothing criminal indicated on their DL history, there's nothing overtly there in the car—there's no odors, no indicators. Simply she's agitated, she's not looking at you. . . .
>
> ENCINIA: [*grunts*] Hmmm. . . .
>
> INTERVIEWER: At what point do you think it becomes unreasonable to detain that person any longer?
>
> ENCINIA: From what we're taught in patrol school, it's a reasonable amount of time that a reasonable officer would use.[79]

The questioner seems dumbfounded. He utters "okay" and just moves on.

But *I* want to linger. *We* have to linger. Because the questioner is not wrong to be confused. Encinia's concern seems to exceed anything reasonable. It seems to exceed reason itself. He's glued there. He cannot leave. Something about Bland keeps him there.

Perhaps this *something* is religious. We know it's affective. But it's the unreasonable nature of his pursuit, his lingering, that raises the question of religion, and specifically religious experience.

Religious studies has often turned to feeling to discuss religious experience. Now, such discussions seem to be no longer useful; we've traded in the term *feeling* for other terms: *power, economics, history, class*. And this is all for good reason: the affective tradition of religious studies failed to acknowledge the political realities of affect, of feeling.[80] But feeling need not be metaphysical. One shouldn't assume that religious experience necessarily distracts us from the very real world of violence, power, and discrimination.

Scholars also have affective language for what Encinia was experiencing.[81] Some might call it the sacred. Others might call it a "feeling of absolute dependence."[82] But perhaps the most famous and infamous philosophical approach to religious experience was Rudolf Otto's. His notion of the *mysterium tremendum et fascinans* describes religious experience as the perception and apprehension of something that is simultaneously terrifying and alluring. It exceeds reason; it is suprarational. It is overwhelming; it overtakes the experiencing subject's sense of their own existence (Otto called it a "creature-feeling").[83]

It is possible, then—indeed, it is very probable—that what kept Encinia at the scene, what gripped him and didn't let him go, was the affective compulsion of perceiving a wholly other reality. Encinia expected docility; Bland was assertive. Encinia expected acquiescence; Bland answered him without reservation and without pleasantries. She didn't look at him. She didn't acknowledge him. But he wanted her to. He wanted her "demeanor," her "body language," to emote something other than irritation/agitation/ anger/aggravation. He wanted her to be pleasant, to affirm his identity. But she didn't; this was something else. The experience was unbelievable.

He was already lured there; he had no reason to pursue her. He couldn't turn away. This *something else* had defied him. *It*—a black female body— had told him no. The defiance became part of the scene. A person became an *area of concern*. He couldn't abide. The concern was overwhelming. It exceeded reason. It was irreducible to what Encinia was seeing. It was irreducible to what he *could* see. This something else didn't calculate. He couldn't understand it. He didn't know what it was. It was unknown. "It's still the unknown," Encinia claims.

The questioner starts to lose patience. *You could have left*, he might have wondered. *You already knew you were going to give her a warning. It didn't have to go this way. But you stayed.* Then the questioner starts wondering aloud: Why did you stay? And why didn't you ask anything other than "are you okay," then?[84] Encinia responds, but what he says is absurd: "I was checking for her well-being, trying to establish a rapport, allow her to vent if she needs to vent, and then we can move on."[85]

The response is so absurd it is almost laughable. In fact, it was laughable: the questioner, now completely lost, chuckles, and then asks, "Do you really, at this point, think she wants to build a rapport with you?"

ENCINIA: I'm not sure, sir.

INTERVIEWER: But you knew she was agitated, right?

ENCINIA: That is correct.[86]

There's nothing there to keep Encinia at the scene, save that he knew she was agitated. But, as the questioner continues to assert, agitation isn't really a cause for suspicion—or at least it shouldn't be. But Encinia doesn't see it this way. He's concerned. He can't shake the concern; he can't leave the scene. He is undone.[87]

Even retrospectively, he's undone. He's bereft of reason, of reasons. "If you thought something was going on [before you asked her to get out of the car]," the questioner asks, "why didn't you ask any further questions?" Encinia's reply: "I'm not sure."[88]

To recap, then: Encinia follows Bland because he cannot determine whether she ran a public or private stop sign; he follows. He's already concerned; he stops her. She isn't pleasant with him; he remains concerned. He goes back to his car, and, having already determined in advance that he's going to give her a warning, he watches her. There's nothing on her driving record, but she moves—too much—in her car. He's even more concerned. He comes back; she's still pissed. The concern heightens. "I don't know what happened, but something did," he says.[89]

But he doesn't say anything. Or rather, he repeats the same question: "What's wrong?" The concern must have been so intense that it robbed him of his ability to articulate. He's lost language.[90] This is a religious experience. And Encinia wasn't ready. He was on edge. All he needed was for something to tip him over.

He asks her to put out her cigarette.

She says no.

There it is. "Well you can go ahead and get out the car now," Encinia demands. He couldn't do anything with her agitation, but that refusal gets him in. He tells her he's going to "light her up" with the taser. She asks—six times—why she's being detained, but that no longer matters—her screams, her pleas, none of it. "My focus was to get her controlled," he says, "what she said or didn't say." It's all unnecessary at that point. The reductive work begins—or it continues. His lingering has paid off. He could regain control of the situation. And he did.

Otto wanted his phenomenology of religious experience to highlight the annihilation of the subject's primacy. And it does. The experiencing subject is at the behest of the wholly other sacredness with which it comes in contact. But it also secures the subject's being. Otto's *mysterium tremendum* may not be Aquinas's unmoved mover, but it does give the subject its reason for life, movement, and being. And while this may work for burning bushes and mystics (and even the mystic is under question for Otto), the normative subject doesn't suffer annihilation so well. Pornographic Affect isn't about subjective annihilation. The "ascetic who aspires to feel nothing," who lives in a world of "flattened affect," is therefore after their own security.

(All modes of asceticism don't function this way, of course; as Niki Clements argues, asceticism can and will invoke affective, embodied, and practical modes of engagement that lean further into sociality and community, and provide powerful possibilities for different modalities of subject formation.[91] But, I think, Lorde's point is that a particular kind of asceticism—one that Clements and others rigorously criticize—is so beholden to notions of affect-free and endless work that they become flattened out. The removal from the messiness of the social world isn't an entrance into another kind of messy and generative sociality; it is, instead, a Weberian compulsion to secure oneself in this world by removing oneself from it. This kind of asceticism, I think, is precisely what Lorde criticizes.)

Encinia's multiple decisions, then, were in favor of reestablishing his centrality. The religious experience had overtaken him: bereft of language, undone by Bland's assertiveness, Encinia did all he could to regain control over a concerning situation.

This shouldn't come as a surprise. *Mysterium tremendum*s are not simply the stuff of burning bushes. Encinia's treatment of Bland has a history. It has histories. These histories are racialized. And they are gendered. Some of them have names: Harriet Jacobs, Patsey, Saartjie Baartman. Others are lost to the violence of anonymity that permeates the archive. But they, all of them, are stories of simultaneous attraction and repulsion. They are encounters that exceed reason. They are stories of compulsion; they were Affective. They are made from black female flesh registering the wounding of pornographically being turned into pornotroped bodies.

Religious experience, then, can be brutal. It can be violent. Otto's formulations remain with us, though not how he might like. The sacred isn't always pleasant.

In fact, it rarely is. Undone and beholding a sacredness before which he was temporarily helpless, bereft of appropriate words and disoriented by Bland's assertiveness, Encinia reduced Bland to an object of *his* sensation; she was there to confirm *his* affects. Bland made Encinia. Unmoved by him, she moved him. She called *him* into being as one who needed a black female body to secure his own subjectivity as an officer of the state. Encinia retroactively deemed Bland combative after the fact. She was there for *him*. He needed her to *be* combative so that his concern would have merit. Everything returned to him. Feedback. Pornography.

Pornographic Affect, then, names a diffuse, experiential, and religious modulation of engagement that denies the complex and multifaceted ways in which blackness, black flesh, lives, responds, and moves through the world. Sandy *died* because of Affect. And trust: it was religious—in the worst way. It still is.

Conclusion: Sandy Still Speaks

But Sandy still speaks. She still shows her love. While Bland may have found herself on the nastiest side of a pornographically affective encounter, she nevertheless loved, cared, smiled, and respected those with whom she came in contact. "Love y'all" was her refrain; and we cannot forget that.

Encinia nevertheless pornographically pornotroped her. He reduced her to an object of excitable irritation in that encounter. Gripped by Bland's irritation that, in turn, became his concern, Encinia reinforced an affective matrix of overdetermined black bodies. The bail system reinforced this matrix by keeping Sandy in jail. She died. There's no way to make light of this. There are no silver linings. Sandy's death remains a horrible tragedy; this violence cannot be undone. And neither should it be overlooked.

That's the thing with flesh, though. It's fragile. It carries the capacity for love and care even as it is visited by the worst and most lethal, brutal, and heinous forms of violence. The yonder remains.

But so does the Clearing. They both remain. Flesh, black flesh, is present in both—and sometimes they occur at the same time. Rhys sat in front of the jail and inspired all of us. We came. We made it through. We laughed. We cried. We danced. And in the midst of this, there were batons waiting. The officers came for us. They disrupted the Clearing we'd enacted. The yonder can and will come.

But this is what it means to be flesh. Bland's life—as is the case with all of us, I would argue—was marked by complex interactions, encounters, and relations with others. The complications are manifold; on the one hand, this is the case because flesh is visited by the yonder. On the other hand, it is complicated because flesh, black flesh, itself is complicated. Bland loved, and her love is complicated. But, though it was complicated, it was nevertheless steeped in sharing feelings. She shared her feelings with her community. Deeply.

I gotta be honest with you guys. I am suffering from something that some of you all may be dealing with right now. It's a little bit of depression as well as PTSD. I've been really stressed out over these past couple of weeks, but that does not excuse me not keeping my promise to you all by letting you know that somebody cares about you, someone loves you and that you can go out there and do great things. . . . If there are any of you that are dealing with these same things . . . it's okay. It's okay to talk about it. . . . I deal with it, and some of you probably deal with it, too, and you have to know that it's okay.[92]

Bland shared her feelings. She invited us to share in them, too. She shared the wonderful ones and the unpleasant ones. But even when reflecting upon her own depression, she still took the time to say, "Someone loves you." She reiterated it in her next video:

On my last video, I did speak on depression, and I want you guys to know it's a daily struggle. It's a daily test. You get up every day, and it depends on how you feel when you wake up that determines how your day is going to go. But I'm here to tell somebody: don't let the depression get you down. Do not let it hold you and keep you locked in the spot where you are.[93]

Bland named her stress and her depression. She shared her own struggles. In so doing, she shared her capacity to love. She told her viewers that somebody loves them. Maybe her *you* could also be an address beyond the intentions and identity of the addresser. Maybe because she still speaks, her love, too, can hint at the capaciousness of the erotic. She shared—what she experienced, what she felt.

Feelings are important. They are shaped by lives. They shape lives. They matter.

Stanley-Jones, Rice, Sterling, and Bland did not always live their lives in relation to the violence visited upon them. They lived beyond their bodies; they lived as flesh, black flesh, which means they lived, moved, felt beyond the subject. They may not still be with us. But their lives—not simply their deaths—tell us much, resonate within us. While their deaths matter to the world and its subjects, conditioning both, their lives continue to matter to those who know otherwise possibilities are present.

The "Sandy Speaks" videos will not bring Bland back. But they resonated. And they resonate. Those videos inspired erotic action. They still do. Sandy spoke. She still speaks. So do all the others.

Love y'all.

CONCLUSION

BLACK LIFE MATTER

A few years ago, when I'd just started my job, I was told by a white scholar that my work was "temporally bound," by which he meant that my work had a shelf life. I can't remember how this scholar specifically phrased it, but the point was clear: my work needed to get out *now*; people wouldn't be interested in a text like this after the BLM era had ended. This was at least three years ago.

I suspect this scholar wasn't alone in his observation. For many, this book will have come too late. "National conversations on race and racism" will have happened; reforms will have been made. Antiracism™ books will have been written; certain writers will have emerged as "leading voices," padding their pockets and expanding their cultural capital in the process. Corporations will have plastered Black Lives Matter all over their respective brands; Black History Month will have become an American meme. Money will have been donated; political campaigns will have come and gone. By the time this book reaches you, it will have long missed its market date. It will have come too late.

What a crock of shit.

The brutally undeniable, long-standing, and enduring reality is that black lives have been, are, and will continue to be sacrificed on the altar of American religion. This hasn't changed. Black death is part of the game. It *is* the game.

For subjects, black death is a (sometimes) terrible but (always) tolerable reality. In fact, it's more than tolerable; it's desired. It's necessary. "The ongoing state-sanctioned legal and extralegal murders of Black people are normative and, for this so-called democracy, necessary," Christina Sharpe writes.[1] Subjects need police because police keep the norms in place. They reinforce the necessary antiblackness that makes this world work. Subjects are too polite to be honest, though, so they turn to other discourses—much of which is religious—to articulate their antiblack compulsions.

What I have tried to show in this text is how black lives speak, and speak back, to theoretical and philosophical treatments of religion, experience, and subjectivity, and how these treatments are inherently antiblack. In chapter 1, I suggested that they turn the problem of evil into a modality of instrumental reason; chapter 2 disclosed how police are interpellated by black flesh, which, in turn, prompts the enactment of deonto(theo) logical duty. Chapter 3 showed that blackness is experienced as a terrifying sacredness that becomes the phenomenological *causa sui*, the "unmoved mover," for the subject. In sitting with these lives, I have tried to show how the subject's self-image and self-fashioning is a religious endeavor through and through. The game of normativity is, in the end, a religious and philosophical one.

I wrote this book as part of a collective effort to end this game. I doubt this dynamic will end in my lifetime. But part of the task of writing is to provide perspective and, perhaps, to offer possibilities. This book has tried to show both. It has tried to show how normative subject formation is antiblack by necessity. And it has also tried to show that blackness still *lives* beyond antiblackness.

At this point, it should be clear that *beyond* is not meant to invoke something like overcoming or escape. *Beyond* doesn't "transcend" or relativize violence. It only underscores the fact that antiblackness is not the whole story (even if it might be the whole game). My understanding of beyond is closer to what Ashon Crawley calls "otherwise possibilities"—possibilities that do not negate the violence of this world, but nevertheless show how blackness *lives* in the midst of violence. To move beyond the world is to be in the Clearing; it is to enact love and care for black flesh. But this love and care happens *in the midst of* this world. Clearings are fragile; the yonder always remains. Violence can continue to happen. Chances are, it will. So, as I said in the introduction: do not mistake my claims or my intentions. Love and care do not erase or escape the violence.

But they are ways that we *live* in the midst of such violence.

To be living matter is to still be living. It is life. And this form of life—a life excluded from the domain of normative subjecthood, and therefore beyond it—is worth tending to. It is worth sitting with.

In order to show this, I have one last story to tell. It is painful. And it is personal. But it is also filled with love and care.

* * *

On February 5, 2016, I sat in the Station Museum, crying uncontrollably.[2] As Nina Simone sang "Strange Fruit" and "Feeling Good," pictures of a proud mother with her son and grandson populated a projector screen. The mother's son's eyes stared back at me from the screen as if they were my own, piercing me with a kind of peace that was almost biblical. He had sleepy eyes, the kind that conveyed confidence. And he was handsome, with the kind of smile that comes with warm, comforting laughter—the subtle kind of laughter that puts you at ease. In the pictures, he was happy.

But that was only one side of the story. We were celebrating the son's birthday, but he wasn't with us. Jordan Baker Sr. had died two years earlier, on January 26, 2014, having been snatched away from his mother, Janet, and his son, Jordan, by a trigger-happy off-duty police officer named Juventino Castro.[3] Deemed suspicious because he was wearing a hoodie while riding his bike past a strip mall, Jordan was chased and then killed by Castro in a back alley.[4] Castro, like the other officers I've chronicled in this project, was not indicted for any criminal charges.[5] I cried uncontrollably because I saw myself in Jordan, a young black man who could at any time be snatched away from my family and friends.

Injustice is often talked about in the abstract, even—and especially—when we discuss particular instances of murder and death. The news outlets report police shootings as if all the victims are the same—some unknown "unarmed black male or female." We speak of injustice in terms of "breathless numbers": 116 people killed by Houston Police Department officers in eleven years with zero charges.[6] The stories run together, numbing us to the real human cost of a lost daughter or son, husband or wife, fiancée, cousin, or sister. The deaths pile up, becoming so heavy that our individual and collective psyches struggle to stand under their weight.[7] And every time we hear about another death, we all die just a little more. I cried because

I saw myself in Jordan—because, even though I knew it wasn't the case, I nevertheless felt as though Jordan's life and death were my own.

As the slideshow ended, Janet, the woman who had survived the loss of her son, took the podium and began to tell us *her* story—the story of a mother who had lost her son too soon and for no reason. She didn't speak in the language of the media—her story didn't include "unarmed black male killed by police" or "police brutality." Her story wasn't sensationalized. She didn't walk us through the "objective prose" of those journalists who have no investment in or concern for the ones who have been lost.[8] Janet only cared about broken relationships, particularly the relationships between a mother and son and father and son that were severed behind the cowardice of a man who thought his badge was a license to kill.

Janet isn't a loud woman; she isn't theatrical. Despite the loss she's suffered, she is remarkably calm when she expresses herself. This may be due to the fact that she is a woman of faith who will quickly and frequently retreat to her prayer closet when life gets hard. Janet's calmness is a testament to her faith.

As she took the podium, she spoke in hushed tones. We had to move the microphone closer to her mouth so that we could all hear what she had to say. But the words she spoke pierced the hearts of anyone who could hear her voice. When she spoke of her grandson, Little Jordan, who had lost his hero, she raised a question that still rings in my ears: "How do you tell your grandson that his superhero has been shot down?" She wondered aloud why she had been inducted "into a sorority that I never pledged for and never wanted to be in," and tried to wrap her head around the grief she was experiencing. Tears streaming down her face, she reminded us that we have words like *widow*, *widower*, and *orphan*, but we "have no word for a parent who has lost their child." She spoke of the limbo she lives on a daily basis, reminding us that grief has no timeline, and that the loss of a son is a debt that cannot be repaid.

Ethicist Katie Cannon once wrote that black women have displayed and continue to display "unshouted courage," the kind of courage that requires no attention even as it keeps the wheels of life moving.[9] This courage isn't strong in the masculine sense. Janet is a fighter, but she isn't pugilistic. She didn't advocate for the kind of coercive power intrinsic to patriarchal forms of expression. Creating a clearing similar to the one in *Beloved*, Janet closed her talk in hopeful tones, telling us that prayer could and would change the situation and bring justice to her family for Jordan's cause. And, as the faith-filled woman she is, she invited us into her prayer closet.

We accepted.

We laid hands on Janet, praying with and for her, holding her up in the collective flesh filling the room. Atheists, humanists, agnostics, Christians, and Muslims laid hands on a childless mother who held us as we held onto her. Janet prophetically glued us together through a vulnerability shot through with love, opening a clearing where not only could we love our own hands, feet, eyes, livers, lungs, and hearts, but we could love hers as well.

Since Janet gave her talk, I have gotten to know her more. She has not fully gotten over her grief. But to be honest, I'm not sure what it would mean to "get over" the loss of a child. That grief remains.

But her joy remains, too. We have laughed together; one of her favorite songs is "Hell You Talmbout" by Janelle Monae, and we have listened to the song together often. She told me this song brings her joy because they mention her son in the lyrics. It brings her joy to know that someone—let alone a celebrity—has taken the time to mention her son. That song, as far as I can tell, is an act of care for Janet.

I am not Janelle Monae. I do not have that kind of musical artistry. But this project is my way of showing that care, too. I wrote this project out of care for the lives that were lost. I also wrote it for Janet and others like her; I wrote it for those who create clearings in the midst of sorrow, for those who know that the Clearing is a temporary, improvised, fragile, and irruptive space.

I want to be clear, though: the Clearing doesn't negate the violence of antiblackness. I tell this story not to garner some kind of liberal sentiment but to announce that, though we live in and through that violence, something beyond the violence remains. As Fred Moten once said, "Troubled air gets out."[10] That air will always be troubled. But it still gets out. And that "getting out" matters. It signals something. I make no claims to fully know what this something is. But I can gesture toward what it might signal— for me, and perhaps for others. I'd like to suggest that this something else points to how we might understand ethics—an ethics of love and care steeped in practice.

* * *

Janet prays regularly; prayer is a practice. It is her practice. She has made it hers; she is contemplative. She is quiet. And in that contemplative quietude, she finds resources for compassion, care, and generosity.

I do not mean to lionize her. I do not mean to romanticize her. But, having gotten to know Janet, having spoken to her on the phone and sat with her in person, I am struck by her tone of voice, by the way she hums her words. Janet does not speak sentences; she unfolds them. She is careful. And this carefulness becomes a way for her to hold her anger and her compassion, her grief and—when she can cultivate it—her laughter.

And yet, none of this stops Janet from being pissed or upset. There is a resilience here—one that informs her engagement with the Houston Police Department, who has still kept Jordan's killer, Juventino Castro, on the force.[11] The city of Houston might have settled with her, but I know that money is not what Janet was after. So, she still fights. She still moves. She still engages. Steeped in the practice of prayer, Janet remains hopeful, caring, and loving. She remains engaged.

Janet is not alone. As I mentioned in chapter 3, people like Rhys Caraway cultivated the practice of sitting vigil in the heat of summer in front of the Waller County jail. In the wake of death, black flesh comes to care, and it does so through practices—many of which we might call spiritual.

I want to linger on practice for a moment. I want to tease out its ethical implications. My teacher, Niki Kasumi Clements, highlights the ethical dimensions and possibilities of practice as a way to navigate political unrest. She points to practice as a way for people to cultivate dispositions that help them make sense of their lives.[12] And this work is ethical; it is a "mode of action open to subjects that are discursively shaped but also capable of self-shaping."[13] Ethics is about how we shape ourselves—and how we do so in community, *with* others.

Clements uses the term *ethics* to describe the work of self-shaping. R. A. Judy uses another term: *poiesis*. With Judy, we are prompted to sit with the "thousand and one little actions that make up a life" as the work of the flesh, as a kind of poiesis that cannot be captured within dominant intellectual schemas. Drumming, dancing, moving; these actions, these decisions, are the way black life shapes itself—and, in turn, the world.[14]

This is what I see in Janet, in Rhys, and in the movement. I see the marches, protests, and direct actions as practices, as a "thousand and one little actions that make up a life," that cultivate a sociality, a modality of collective living, that allows people to find possibility, meaning, joy, and love in the midst of violence. As I sat with my community who advocated for Bland, as we organized in the name of a woman who loved her community, and as I sat with Janet, I realized that, although we will not win every battle, we had each other.

This doesn't stop the work. And it does not end the violence. We can and will die. We can and will suffer. Antiblackness prevails. And—*and*—we still have each other. Like Fred Moten, I am in profound agreement with Afropessimist thinkers about the social death of blackness. I concede that this world is semantically, grammatically, and ontologically structured as antiblack. Having each other will not cancel out the ongoing, overwhelming, soul-withering, and flesh-dehiscing violence that is antiblackness. There is no way out of that. Not anytime soon, anyway. I would hope that no one would read this text and assume that I am possessed by some kind of naive optimism. That would be far from the case.

But in a world like this, love, sociality, and care matter. They are meaningful. They are not to be overemphasized. But they sustain. They hold us. We enact them; they are ethical. Love and care are ethical capacities. And they show themselves through practices.

* * *

Some will say that my emphasis on care returns us to a liberal humanist project. They might hear the word *care* and think about Heidegger. And if I were drawing from Heidegger, they would be right: Heideggerian care, *Zorge*, is the care of a *Dasein* who, in its self-centeredness, can work out the meaning of its being only through use and through its attempts to overcome death. That kind of care invokes the violence of the ship *Zorgue*, the ship named "care," that would throw its "cargo" overboard in the name of "lightening" its load.[15] *Zorgue/Zorge* is steeped in metaphysics, a care that must be resolute in its vigilance in overcoming death. This resoluteness entails displacing that death onto others, onto blackness. This dynamic remains; it isn't going anywhere.

While such a reading would be appropriate, it would also be insufficient. And, in an ironic twist, it would be too Heideggerian. This kind of reading would betray its allegiance to the very structure of thought it seeks to deconstruct; having become so faithful to Heidegger, a reading like this would dismiss how black life is irreducible to the metaphysical nothingness of Heideggerian thought. For all of its contributions, black nihilism is a bridge too far for me. It's too steeped in the very metaphysics against which it (thinks it) militates; it takes the word of metaphysical thinkers too seriously; it misses the richness of black life in its desire to explicate the truth of black nothingness. Heideggerian care isn't the only care operative. The care of which I speak is not beholden to *Zorgue/Zorge*.

I keep returning to this question Christina Sharpe asked: "How can we think (and rethink and rethink) care laterally, in the register of the intramural, in a different relation than that of the violence of the state? In what ways do we remember the dead, those lost in the Middle Passage, those who arrived reluctantly, and those still arriving?"[16] To "think (and rethink and rethink) care laterally" is an ongoing project. It is a process of constant remembering; it is a continual visioning and re-visioning of our capacities to hold and remember one another even as we live and die in the perpetual hold. It is to tend to a mystical rubbing—of bodies together, of arms locked together, of feet scraping asphalt.[17] I have chronicled the subject-forming capacities of antiblack violence in this book. But I have also gestured toward the ways that black flesh cares. Care is enfleshed. It is engaged. It acts.

This kind of care, lateral in its direction and intramural in its scope, is about neither use nor a vigilance against death. Such use would be ineffective; such vigilance would be misplaced. After all, we are already dead. That we are sentient doesn't change that fact. We are always dying. "It is always now," Beloved tells us.

Beloved keeps trying to care, though. She wants to bite away the chains of bondage. And it's important to note: she cannot do it. It is not possible. But she still desires to do so. And that desire, that push for something like liberation through care, is ethical. Beloved shapes, and is shaped by, the love she has for the woman who shares her face. And, for me, this signals an ethical disposition. Care matters. "Remembering the dead" matters. Janet remembers Jordan. Mertilla remembers Aiyana. Samaria remembers Tamir. Quintilla and Cameron remember Alton. Geneva remembers Sandy. Mothers, communities, and activists remember their dead. The movement is a movement of care, of remembrance. And in caring, in remembering, it envisions and enacts a deathly life where such death would not continue to come so quickly and so pervasively.

* * *

As I conclude, I would like to say, too, that ethics are not simply about the intramural capacities for shaping individual and collective lives. Part of the reason why I wrote this book is to show how ethics is about those normative structures of violence that also make lives. *Antiblackness is as ethical as intramural care.* It is the way subjects make sense of themselves. It is the lens through which subjects take action, the condition through which their formation unfolds. Aiyana and Tamir make Joseph Weekley and Timothy Loehmann possible; Alton calls Blane Salamoni and Howie Lake II into being; Sandy moved Encinia affectively and prompted his violence. And all of these lives contribute to a national ethos of denigrating and eliminating black life in the name of a national project. Their lives mattered. They still matter. Even to those who would say otherwise.

But they also matter to me, to us, to those of us who remember them. And they matter differently. They matter to me, to us, as *living* matter, as flesh, that resonates in and beyond their deaths. Aiyana loved Disney princesses; Tamir loved to make people laugh. Alton loved music; Sandy loved the children.

These four black lives mattered.

In fact, they still matter.

The question before us, then, is how we might live in light of their memory.

Notes

INTRODUCTION

1. Although this story haunts me, I am forever indebted to Janet Baker, the mother of Jordan Baker, for her grace and invitation to participate in a radio show where we spoke with family members who had lost loved ones to police officers. To Janet: thank you. I will never forget your unshouted courage, your quiet grace. I am in awe of your compassion, your strength, and who you are in general.

2. Lane, "Alton Sterling and His CD-Selling Gig."

3. Heidegger, *Being and Time*, section on "The They" (particularly 149–57).

4. Heidegger critiqued inauthentic engagement. But he didn't deny it and—contrary to standard readings—neither did he find it to be problematic. It was just limited in allowing *Dasein* to clarify its own being-in-the-world.

5. Sharpe, *In the Wake*, 10.

6. Sharpe, *In the Wake*, 18.

7. Sharpe, *In the Wake*, 38–42.

8. For more on hatred, see Ahmed, *The Cultural Politics of Emotion*, particularly the chapter "Organisation of Hate."

9. Sharpe, *In the Wake*, 5.

10. Lewis Gordon gifted me with the phrase "philosophical eulogy." For that, and for his work and support of me and my project, I am grateful.

11. Hartman, *Lose Your Mother*, 6.

12. Sharpe, *In the Wake*, 14.

13. For those phenomenologically inclined, this line is a direct criticism of Heidegger's notion of *Zorge*—care—as that notion of care is steeped in *Dasein's* own existential possibilities and limitations. Heideggerian care has everything to do with the normative subject's self-investments; it is a navel-gazing approach wherein *Dasein* concerns itself with itself—with its own life and death. For more on this, see Heidegger, *Being and Time*.

14. Recently, one of my beloveds had a life-and-death health crisis. In the midst of COVID-19, I was unable to visit them. But I was able to use Facetime to see them in the hospital. This method is as personal as it is conceptual.

15. I really hope my words don't do more damage. But I cannot determine how this book will be read.

16. Zakiyyah Jackson makes a beautiful and powerful case for why "inclusion into the human" offers little to no solace for black life. See Jackson, *Becoming Human*, particularly the introduction.

17. Hartman, *Scenes of Subjection*, 3–4.

18. Hartman, *Scenes of Subjection*.

19. Moten, *In the Break*, 4.

20. Hartman enacts perhaps one of the most famous omissions—or, more precisely and as Fred Moten calls it, "repressions"—in black studies: namely, she represses the story of Aunt Hester's beating at the beginning of Frederick Douglass's *Narrative*. And she does so for reasons I've outlined in the text. But Fred Moten raises a point that also cannot be dismissed: "Like Douglass, [Hartman] transposes all that is unspeakable in the scene to later, ritualized, 'soulfully' mundane and quotidian performances. All that's missing is the originary recitation of the beating, which she reproduces in her reference to it. This is to say that there is an intense dialogue with Douglass that structures *Scenes of Subjection*. The dialogue is opened by a refusal of recitation that reproduces what it refuses." In other words, repressing the narrative does not necessarily stave off the possibility of enjoyment, nor does it stem the tide of the violence. The possibility—for enjoyment, for more violence—remains. And so the question is, as I say in the introduction, how we might handle these stories. Sitting-with is my "how." And I say more about it in this section. For more on this, see Moten, *In the Break*, 5.

21. Moten, *In the Break*, 5.

22. Many black studies scholars have developed theories of black opacity, but perhaps Edouard Glissant is the most well known. For more on this, see Glissant, *Poetics of Relation*. But here, I'm thinking of Charles Long's notion of opacity as it relates to blackness. In his work, he attunes us to the idea that, at least since modernity, Western knowledge production has understood "transparency as a metaphor for knowledge," and in so doing, it has enacted violence against the "opaque"—or, as Long put it, "dusky"—beings who do not fully show themselves. I'll have more to say on this later. For more on Long's discussion of opacity, see *Significations*.

23. I want to say, here and now, that a significant amount of the royalties (if there are any) from this text will go to the families of the victims I chronicle here. I plan on donating a portion of the proceeds to the Tamir Rice Foundation, as well as to the Sandra Bland Center for Racial Justice.

24. For those who are not scholars or interested in philosophical methodology, I encourage you to read one of the chapters and then return to this section.

25. In "The Case of Blackness," Fred Moten critically reads Frantz Fanon's chapter "The Lived Experience of the Black" as "not only a lament over Fanon's

own relegation to the status of object; [this chapter] also contains a lament that it suppresses over the general annihilation of the thing to which transcendental phenomenology contributes insofar as it is concerned with *Sachen* [things *qua* things], not *Dinge* [things *qua* objects], in what remains untranslatable as its direction toward the things themselves." Moten, "The Case of Blackness," 184.

In other words, Moten claims that phenomenology is preoccupied with the object—which is something subjects represent to themselves—not the thing, which eludes or exceeds the subject's representational capacities. Moten quotes Heidegger as saying, "Man can represent, no matter *how*, only what has previously come to light of its own accord and has shown itself to him in the light it brought with it," and then he elaborates by saying, "For Heidegger, the thingliness of the thing . . . is precisely that which *prompts* its making. For Plato—and the tradition of representational thinking he codifies, which includes Fanon—everything present is experienced as an object of making where 'object' is understood, in what Heidegger calls its most precise expression, as 'what stands forth' (rather than what stands before or opposite or against)" ("Case of Blackness," 183).

I'm laying all of this out because when I say that phenomenology doesn't stay with the experienced, I'm affirming Moten's criticism of phenomenology; while I'm sure that some phenomenologists will claim that Heidegger's discussion of the thing isn't phenomenological—after all, for late Heidegger, there might be nothing more real than *Sachen*, which means that he doesn't bracket or suspend his judgment about the reality of the thing—Moten's criticism is of the phenomenological method. I read him as saying what I say above: phenomenology moves on—to the subject's consciousness, to its capacity to represent. And in so doing, phenomenology doesn't stay with "the things themselves"; it only turns to them as objects available for subjective and transcendental consciousness. Phenomenology moves on. And it is precisely in its moving on that it fails to grasp or behold the irreducible complexity of the things—not the noematic objects— subjects encounter.

26. Husserl, *Cartesian Meditations*, 21, emphasis added.

27. Husserl often conceived of phenomenology as an ethical enterprise of critical self-reflection. To the extent that turning within and bracketing one's assumptions might bring clarity about one's own perspective on the world, classical phenomenology has promise. But to the extent that this clarity comes at the cost of one not attending to the manifold alterity that constitutes the subject's very perspective, the ethical promise of such a method remains in question. For more on this, see the epilogue to Husserl, *Ideas Pertaining to a Pure Phenomenology and a Phenomenological Philosophy*.

28. "The hyletic, which deals with matter," Michel Henry writes, "is not only situated 'far below noetic and functional phenomenology.' It is not simply 'subordinated' to it. To the extent that [the hyletic] only has a signification 'by the fact that it provides possible gussets in the intentional eave, possible matter for intentive formations,' a content for appearing and for the givenness that is the business of intentional phenomenology, hyletic phenomenology is

a phenomenology in the trivial and pre-critical sense of the term." Moreover, "'Sensible givens, sensuous data' must be understood in the sense whereby 'being given as a matter for intentional complexes' is being given *in a certain way*, as something traversed by an intentional regard that casts it before itself and gives it to be seen. The 'sensible appearances' through which the world is given to us *do not give themselves. They are only appearances or phenomena inasmuch as they are animated by a noetic intention and come to appear through it*" (*Material Phenomenology*, 11, emphasis added).

29. Moten, "The Case of Blackness," 182.

30. I am aware of second-person phenomenology. Perhaps the foremost proponent of this is Emmanuel Levinas, who reverses the direction of intentionality to make the other, the second person, primary. For more on this, see Levinas, *Totality and Infinity*.

31. Emphasis added. *Graham v. Connor* was a case in which Dethorne Graham was beaten by M. S. Connor, an officer who deemed Graham's actions suspicious. See "Justia Opinion Summary and Annotations," Justia, US Supreme Court, accessed December 29, 2021, https://supreme.justia.com/cases/federal/us/490/386/ for a synopsis of the case.

32. Perhaps I'm more Derridean than I appear, but my point here is to say that we cannot *not* use language. Even if language is a problem, it is all we have. The issue, then, is how we use this language: Do we take language for granted, presupposing a correlationist theory of truth? Or do we recognize, along with Derrida, that meanings are always in flux—in play, as he would say—and therefore we use language always with an eye toward its limitations and its insufficiencies?

33. Sharpe, *In the Wake*, 46.

34. The phenomenological *epoché* is now famous; Husserl used it to suspend judgment about the reality of a thing in order to understand how one experiences the thing; the early Heidegger used a variant of it to suspend our ontological assumptions about the meaning of being; and the earlier Merleau-Ponty deployed a variant of it to disclose the centrality and importance of the body to the development of subjectivity. While I don't read Levinas as using the *epoché*, I could be mistaken. The *epoché* might be useful in certain contexts, but when it comes to living beings—and here specifically, black lives—such a move is problematic and, quite frankly, unethical. I'll say why later in the section.

35. Sharpe, *In the Wake*, 120.

36. Sharpe, *In the Wake*, 120.

37. "The Other," Levinas writes, "can also not appear without renouncing his radical alterity, without entering into an order. The breaks in the order reenter the order whose weave lasts unendingly, a weave these breaks manifest, and which is a totality. The unwonted is understood. The apparent interference of the Other in the Same has been settled beforehand. The disturbance, the clash of two orders, then does not deserve our attention. *That is, unless one is attached to abstraction.*" Levinas's point here is that there is an irruption that the Other brings, but abstraction denies this irruption its disruptive capacities.

While I do not fully ascribe to Levinas's phenomenology—I think there is a difference between opacity and alterity, as opacity is not the total or absolute unknowability of something, but instead the fugitivity, the perpetual escape, of meaning's grasp—I do think that this irruptive capacity of the Other that Levinas gestures toward produces a methodological maxim to not search for abstraction, to not turn to the development of theory. For more on this, see Levinas, "Enigma and Phenomenon," 68.

38. Long, *Significations*, 207, emphasis added.

39. See Christian, "The Race for Theory," 51.

40. Christian, "The Race for Theory," 51.

41. Nahum Chandler, referenced in Carter, "Paratheological Blackness," 590–91. For those who are familiar with Fred Moten, I am of course referencing his essay "The Case of Blackness," in which he tells us that fugitivity is the movement of blackness. He elaborates, "the problem of the inadequacy of any ontology to blackness, to that mode of being for which *escape or apposition* and not the objectifying encounter with otherness is the prime modality, must be understood in its relation to the inadequacy of calculation to being in general." In other words, the fugitivity of blackness exposes the limitations, the "inadequacies," of dominant modes of thinking that seek to contain and constrain existence—especially black existence. For more on this, see Moten, "The Case of Blackness," 187.

42. Notice that I leave the term *lives* unqualified. I am not interested in espousing an anthropocentric understanding of life. I do handle human lives in this book; those lives are the ones that touched me, that have changed me. My attention is focused on Aiyana, Tamir, Alton, and Sandra. But know that I have a more expansive understanding of *life* than an anthropocentric one might allow.

43. I say "for better or worse" because many different organizations have been incorrectly lumped under its name, and also because the phrase has been instrumentalized, exploited, and commodified nearly beyond recognition by those who refuse its radicality.

44. Makalani, "Black Lives Matter and the Limits of Formal Black Politics," 547.

45. See Taylor, *From #BlackLivesMatter to Black Liberation*; Ransby, *Making All Black Lives Matter*; Lebron, *The Making of Black Lives Matter*. And for the articles, see the special issue of *South Atlantic Quarterly* 116, no. 3 (July 2017); I've already cited Makalani's article above; the title of Debra Thompson's article is "An Exoneration of Black Rage."

46. Jared Sexton's "Unbearable Blackness" has a beautiful line of questioning: "Black Lives Matter: how so and to whom, in what ways and by what means, when and under what conditions, precisely? What, moreover, does it mean to matter at all, much less for a life to matter, for lives to matter, let alone for *black* lives to matter? Do black lives matter only when taken together, or taken apart, or taken apart together? Black lives are (a) strange matter." And it is precisely this parenthetical "a" that announces the polyvalent power of the phrase. See Sexton, "Unbearable Blackness," 159.

47. Moten, *In the Break*, 1.

48. I say "we" because there are so many thinkers who correlate blackness with flesh. I will be specifically referencing Zakiyyah Jackson's brilliant work in this section. But many of those thinkers are drawing from Hortense Spillers's brilliant distinction between body and flesh in "Mama's Baby"; although there are multiple ways to read that distinction, most black studies scholars agree on the complex existence of flesh as engendering the violence of subjection and subjugation even as it is the condition for the dissolution of such violence. As Weheliye claims, flesh is that "ether, that 'shit that make your soul burn slow' as well as a modality of relation" (*Habeas Viscus*, 48).

49. "What we are calling flesh," Merleau-Ponty writes, "has no name in any philosophy. As the formative *medium* of the object and the subject, it is not the atom of being, the hard in itself that resides in a unique place and moment: one can indeed say of my body that it is not elsewhere, but one cannot say that it is *here* or *now* in the sense that objects are; and yet my vision does not soar over them, it is not the being that is *wholly* knowing [emphasis added], for it has its own inertia, its ties" (*Visible and Invisible*, 148).

50. R. A. Judy has just written a magisterial work called *Sentient Flesh: Thinking in Disorder, Poiesis in Black* that discusses the complexities of black flesh and its practices and praxes. I wish I could give it full treatment here, but doing so would be beyond the scope of this book. I do, however, gesture toward it in the conclusion as a way to think about ethics.

51. Maurice Merleau-Ponty tells us that flesh is reversible, which means that it is neither the experiencer nor the experienced, but the condition both occasions and undoes the distinction between the two. He writes,

If we can show that the flesh is an ultimate notion, that it is not the union or compound of two substances, but thinkable by itself, if there is a relation of the visible with itself that traverses me and constitutes me as a seer, this circle which I do not form, which forms me, this coiling over of the visible upon the visible, can traverse, animate other bodies as well as my own. And if I was to be able to understand how this wave arises within me, how the visible which is yonder is simultaneously *my* landscape, I can understand . . . that elsewhere it also closes over upon itself and that there are other landscapes besides my own.

His point in all of this is that flesh doesn't allow for simple distinctions, that the "coiling over" of flesh is precisely what makes one both part of and distinct from other inhabitants of the world. See Merleau-Ponty, *The Visible and the Invisible*, 141.

52. Merleau-Ponty tells us that flesh "has no name in philosophy" (*The Visible and the Invisible*, 148).

53. Spillers, "Mama's Baby," 67. But as the endnotes show, I am also thinking about Merleau-Ponty here. "Yes or no," he asks, "do we have a body—that is, not a permanent object of thought, but a *flesh that suffers when it is wounded, hands that touch*?" According to Merleau-Ponty, flesh occasions relational possibilities through splitting apart; I draw from Spillers to show that this splitting isn't always pleasant or harmonious. See Merleau-Ponty, *The Visible and the Invisible*, 137, 146.

54. I understand Moten's frustration with this line, but to think of blackness as a testament to the fact that "objects can and do resist" is to invoke—as he does later on in that introductory chapter—the inextricable connection between life, materiality, and blackness. Here, I'm interested in criticizing the philosophical structures that engender violence against black life as a condition of possibility for the subject. In making this claim, I'm indebted to a host of black studies scholars—not simply Moten, and too many to name here, but for a brief reference, one might look at Weheliye, *Habeas Viscus*; and Moten, *In the Break*; and for a more religious treatment of this, consider Crawley, *Blackpentecostal Breath*.

55. Jackson, *Becoming Human*, 3.

56. Jackson, *Becoming Human*, 72.

57. Jackson, *Becoming Human*, 71.

58. Jackson, *Becoming Human*, 71, emphasis added; 71, emphasis in original.

59. For those who know, "enframing" (*Gestell*) is Heidegger's name for the instrumental reason that technology enacts. Water is enframed as hydroelectric power; trees are enframed as sources of fuel for fire and paper. Enframing, technology, "challenges" matter to become useful, to become something wholly available for use. See Martin Heidegger, "The Question concerning Technology," in *The Question concerning Technology and Other Essays*.

60. Michael Brown, Sr., and Lesley McSpadden vs. City of Ferguson, Missouri, Former Police Chief Thomas Jackson, and Former Police Officer Darren Wilson, "Defendant Darren Wilson's Responses to Plaintiffs' First Set of Requests for Admissions," December 28, 2016, accessed April 3, 2017, http://apps.washingtonpost .com/g/documents/national/us-district-court-document-including-officer-darren -wilsons-list-of-admissions/2371/.

61. You'll notice that I don't racialize the subject. I don't ascribe it a gender. I also leave questions of class, sexuality, and nationality open. This is intentional: subjects are expressions, embodiments, and beneficiaries of the dominant political, epistemological, philosophical, and religious norms of this world. Subjects are expressions of what Heidegger calls the "they": "This being-with-one-another," Heidegger writes, "dissolves one's own Dasein completely into the kind of Being of 'the Others,' in such a way, indeed, that the Others, as distinguishable and explicit, vanish more and more. In this inconspicuousness and unascertainability, the real dictatorship of the 'they' is unfolded. We take pleasure and enjoy ourselves as *they* take pleasure; we read, see, and judge about literature and art as *they* see and judge; likewise we shrink back from the 'great mass' as *they* shrink back; we find 'shocking' what *they* find shocking. The 'they,' which is nothing definite, and which all are, though not as the sum, prescribes the kind of being of everydayness." Even though straight, white, cisgendered people are the primary embodiments of normative subjectivity, they aren't the only ones; subjects are those beings for whom "the Being of everydayness" takes precedent; they also benefit from this structure as well. See Heidegger, *Being and Time*, 164.

62. Again, Judy's work *Sentient Flesh* comes to mind. He tells us that black flesh occasions a kind of thinking-in-disorder, a mode of thought and praxis that, as

I read him, disrupts the philosophical, theological, scientific, and mathematical foundations of the world.

63. Spillers, "Mama's Baby," 67.

64. Emmanuel Levinas tells us in *Totality and Infinity* that reason emerges as a reflection on one's actions for or against the Other. And in *Otherwise Than Being, or Beyond Essence*, Levinas tells us, "The unlimited responsibility in which I find myself comes from the hither side of my freedom, from a 'prior to every memory,' an 'ulterior to every accomplishment,' from the non-present par excellence, the non-original, the anarchical, prior to or beyond essence." His point here is that, at the end of the day, the subject's responsibility stems from a "null-site of subjectivity," wherein the notion of freedom is already put into question. Subjective freedom comes after. See Levinas, *Otherwise Than Being*, 10.

65. I'm sure that, if he were alive, Emmanuel Levinas would have serious consternations about my claims. After all, for Levinas, ethics is first philosophy; it is his primary word. Ethics exceeds being; it goes beyond it. I don't disagree—in fact, the majority of my attention in this book is devoted to what might be called the ethical implications of that which is beyond the ontological and epistemological capacities of the thinking subject. But where Levinas wants to stay in beyond being, I'd like to claim that the beyond of being nevertheless requires attention to being. And this is the case because my primary phenomenological content is neither the face nor the hostage, but the slave and its afterlives. In sticking with black life, I am beholden to a tradition where personhood was transformed into the brute materiality of the merely corporeal body—which is to say, the objective body. I sit not with faces, but with (the tradition of) objects.

66. In *Being and Time*, Martin Heidegger claims that *Dasein* works out the meaning of its being in and through the projected possibilities it has before it. In this regard, *Dasein* clarifies who and what it is through doing things; one of the first moves of "fundamental ontology" is to realize how practical identity forms the foundation for ontological deliberation.

67. If you're thinking this is a criticism of Cartesian and Husserlian phenomenological philosophy, you'd be right. Descartes wants to claim *cogito ergo sum*, but it turns out that if there is nothing to think about, the cogito doesn't exist. And while Husserl concedes the directionality of thinking as well as the fact that thinking is conditioned by horizons, he nevertheless focuses primarily on the movement of consciousness. In *Cartesian Meditations*, Husserl makes it clear that this world is "for me," by which he means that, even if this world is what I think about, it is nevertheless available to and for my thinking, my determinations, my constitutions.

68. Butler, *Senses of the Subject*, 1.

69. For more on the relationship between religion, blackness, and the imagination of matter, see Noel, *Black Religion and the Imagination of Matter*. See also Pinn, *Terror and Triumph*; as well as Long, "Mircea Eliade and the Imagination of Matter." Though Noel is critical of Pinn's project, Pinn nevertheless articulates black religion as tethered to the history of objects, situating black religion and black religious experience as connected to materiality.

70. In *Authors of the Impossible*, Jeffrey Kripal makes a compelling case for retaining the term *sacred* even as it has been denigrated in religious studies. While I do not share his tendency to emphasize our shared capacities, I am nevertheless deeply informed by and grateful for his insistence that we experience things that exceed reason—and in religious studies, we call those suprarational experiences sacred ones. See the introduction and conclusion to Kripal, *Authors of the Impossible*.

71. Crawley, "Stayed Freedom Hallelujah," 29.

72. Crawley, "Stayed Freedom Hallelujah," 31.

73. In *X: The Problem of the Negro as a Problem for Thought*, Nahum Chandler lays claim to the fact that blackness, black life, is irreducible to a simple binary, even as it nevertheless must work with and within them.

74. Weheliye, *Habeas Viscus*, 54.

75. Crawley, *Blackpentecostal Breath*, 79.

76. Moten, *Black and Blur*, xiii.

77. Sharpe, *In the Wake*, 22, emphasis added.

78. Crawley, *Blackpentecostal Breath*, 3–4.

1. HANDS AND BRAIDS

1. Burns, "Detroit Police Officer Who Shot 7-Year-Old."

2. LeDuff, "What Killed Aiyana Stanley-Jones?"

3. Transcription of Joseph Weekley's testimony, accessed on YouTube (WXYZ-TV Detroit, "Officer on Trial").

4. Joseph Weekley's testimony (WXYZ-TV Detroit, "Officer on Trial").

5. Burns, "Aiyana Jones Trial: Questions and Inconsistencies."

6. Loehmann, "Timothy Loehmann Statement."

7. Loehmann, "Timothy Loehmann Statement," 1.

8. Loehmann, "Timothy Loehmann Statement," 2.

9. Loehmann, "Timothy Loehmann Statement," 1.

10. Loehmann, "Timothy Loehmann Statement," 1–2.

11. For some reason, Loehmann's "we are taught" and "we are trained" reads to me like the "ditto ditto" of the archives in Christina Sharpe's *In the Wake*, 52–58. I can't shake this, and I don't know what to make of the resonance, so I note it here. Perhaps readers will see what I mean.

12. Dewan and Oppel, "In Tamir Rice Case."

13. Flynn, "How to Make a Police Shooting Disappear."

14. Fantz, Almasy, and Shoichet, "Tamir Rice Shooting."

15. Crenshaw and Ritchie, "#SAYHERNAME."

16. Burns, "What the Police Officer Who Killed Philando Castile Said."

17. Abu-Jamal, *Have Black Lives Ever Mattered?*, 24–25.

18. Abu-Jamal, *Have Black Lives Ever Mattered?*, 25.

19. Hartman and Wilderson, "The Position of the Unthought," 184–85. We might also hear hints of a Derridean supplement flowing in and through Wilderson and Hartman's conversation.

20. Hartman, *Scenes of Subjection*, 25.

21. Hartman, *Scenes of Subjection*, 58.

22. Hartman and Wilderson, "The Position of the Unthought," 188–89.

23. One can see this in almost every Husserlian text, but Michel Henry makes this clear in his *Material Phenomenology*, 19.

24. Ahmed, *Queer Phenomenology*.

25. Ahmed, *Queer Phenomenology*, 29–34.

26. Although Henry wants to hold out a minor distinction between sensibility and impressionality, his readings of Husserl take us right to the sensory as the space of the hyletic, of the material—and therefore the impressional.

27. Henry claims that "if 'a complex multiplicity of hyletic data, e.g. color-data, etc., acquire the function of a manifold adumbration of one and the same objective physical thing,' it is because these data are presented in a certain way. . . . It is because their appearing *obeys an organization* on which the synthetic unities and the objective order itself are modeled and based" (*Material Phenomenology*, 20).

28. Henry, *Material Phenomenology*, 22.

29. Fred Moten and Ashon Crawley have testified to the fact that blackness is a tradition that "inheres in objects"; black life is forced to reckon with the violently objectifying rules of a subjective consciousness. See Moten, *In the Break*; and Crawley, *Blackpentecostal Breath*.

30. Fanon, *Black Skin, White Masks*, 89.

31. Butler, *Bodies That Matter*, 2.

32. Husserl, *The Crisis of European Sciences*, 107.

33. This seems to be, in part, what Fanon was after when he invoked the racial-epidermal schema as a phenomenological encounter with blackness. Casting "an objective gaze" over his own features (and the term *gaze* is important here—it names sight as a mode of engagement), Fanon begins to see the significations and figurations placed upon him without his permission. He is a "Negro," a "dirty nigger," and there is little he can do about this; he was seen this way long before he was born. The "Negro" in "Look, a Negro!" is therefore a material phenomenology of blackness as sensation, of blackness perceived through the senses. See Fanon, *Black Skin, White Masks*, 89.

34. I am aware that I devote a lot of space to sight in this section. But I hope it is clear that I am criticizing sight's centrality rather than advocating for it. Mark Smith tells us that ocularcentrism has dominated the history of the senses, particularly due to the philosophical reliance on sight as the portal to thinking. My goal here is to show that sight can and will entail violence. See Smith, *Sensing the Past*.

35. Loehmann, "Timothy Loehmann Statement."

36. Goff et al., "The Essence of Innocence." Goff et al. used the following tools to conduct their research: (1) age assessment tasks that prompted participants to identify the perceived age of children of various races; (2) a "culpability scale" that used questions like, "How responsible is [a person] for [that person's] actions" to assess how participants perceived culpability in children of various races; (3) "Implicit Association Tasks" (IATs) that exposed unknown and unintentional

associations of race with "positive" or "negative" realities; (4) an "Attitude Toward Blacks" (ATB) scale that raised questions about explicit racial prejudice—such as, "It is likely that Blacks will bring violence to neighborhoods when they move in"; and (5) a "Dehumanization IAT" that assessed participants' unconscious associations of children with stereotypical representations (like associating a black child with an ape) or violence. See Goff et al., "The Essence of Innocence," 530–31.

37. Goff et al., "The Essence of Innocence," 541.

38. Goff et al., "The Essence of Innocence," 540.

39. Curran, *The Anatomy of Blackness*, 1–2.

40. Curran, *The Anatomy of Blackness*, 118–30.

41. Curran, *The Anatomy of Blackness*, 2, 125.

42. Smith, *How Race Is Made*.

43. Smith, *How Race Is Made*, 1.

44. Koenig, "Misdemeanor, Meet Mr. Lawsuit."

45. Koenig, "Misdemeanor, Meet Mr. Lawsuit."

46. Koenig, "Misdemeanor, Meet Mr. Lawsuit."

47. I know the term *malediction* means something closer to "speaking evil of," but I'm drawing closer to the etymology of the word roots.

48. Spillers, "Mama's Baby," 64.

49. Long, *Significations*, 4.

50. Long, *Significations*, 4–5.

51. Spillers, "Mama's Baby," 65.

52. Spillers, "Mama's Baby," 65, emphasis added.

53. Spillers, "Mama's Baby," 67.

54. Warren, *Ontological Terror*, 45.

55. Warren, *Ontological Terror*, 45. See also Heidegger, *Being and Time*, 89–102.

56. Heidegger, *Being and Time*, 95–104.

57. See Hartman's analysis of the slave as fungible in *Scenes of Subjection*, 21–26.

58. Spillers, "Mama's Baby," 67.

59. Here we would do well to realize that movements like #SayHerName, as well as the report that carries this phrase as its title, make clear that black women are just as subject to state-sanctioned violence as their male counterparts. Although I focus on Mertilla and Samaria in this section, I want to reiterate: thoughtlessness killed Aiyana and Tamir. Aiyana's purported gender made no difference in the state's determinations of the officers' fates.

60. Bukowski, "Detroit Mourns Aiyana Jones."

61. Anderson, "Aiyana's Slaying a Slip of the Trigger?"

62. Anderson, "Aiyana's Slaying a Slip of the Trigger?"

63. Burns, "How Aiyana Jones' Grandmother Didn't Help."

64. Spillers, "Mama's Baby," 67.

65. Spillers, "Mama's Baby," 78.

66. Blackwell, "Lawyer Representing Tamir Rice's Family Defended Boy's Mom"; Johnson, "#Tamir Rice Mom Had Illegal Weapon Charge, Criminal Record," wherein Johnson not only says, "Rice's reported dealings with the criminal justice

system didn't set a good example for her now deceased son," but also lists mugshots and court records of Samaria's cases.

67. This overdetermination extended at least as recently as 2016, when a Cleveland Municipal School District resource officer called Samaria a "stupid bitch" because Tamir was killed. Sheryl Estrada reported the story at *DiversityInc*: "School District Employee Calls Tamir Rice's Mom 'Stupid B**ch.'"

68. Brown, *The Repeating Body*.

69. Brown, *The Repeating Body*.

70. Spillers, "Mama's Baby," 66.

71. In the introduction to *Bodies That Matter*, Butler alerts us to the fact that a "constitutive outside" is how matter gets configured. For more on this, we might also turn to Christina Sharpe, who articulates blackness as a constitutive outside through its trans* presence from modernity moving forward (*In the Wake*, 30).

72. Kelly Brown Douglas, James Cone, Anthony Pinn, and M. Shawn Copeland all speak to the theological dimensions of black bodies. See Douglas, *What's Faith Got to Do with It?*, as well as *Stand Your Ground*; Cone, *The Cross and the Lynching Tree*; Pinn, *Embodiment and the New Shape of Black Theological Thought*; and Copeland, *Enfleshing Freedom*.

73. See Gordon, "Race, Theodicy, and the Normative Emancipatory Challenges of Blackness."

74. Ross, "Police Officers Convicted for Fatal Shootings Are the Exception."

75. Lind, "The FBI Is Trying to Get Better Data." Wesley Lowery also reports similar findings: see "A Disproportionate Number of Black Victims."

76. Long, *Significations*, 7.

77. Ahmed, *Queer Phenomenology*, 7.

78. Ahmed, *Queer Phenomenology*, 7.

79. Long, *Significations*, 7.

80. Spillers, "Mama's Baby," 67.

81. Crawley, *Blackpentecostal Breath*, 78–79, emphasis added.

82. Zielinski, "Protesters Shut Down Streets."

83. Weheliye, *Habeas Viscus*, 43.

2. "WHAT I DO?"

1. Department of Justice, "Federal Officials Close Investigation into Death of Alton Sterling."

2. I do not recommend watching the videos. I have had to do so. Multiple times. And every time, I shudder at the end.

3. CBS News, "Alton Sterling Shooting."

4. CBS News, "Alton Sterling Shooting."

5. Massumi, "The Future Birth of the Affective Fact," 55.

6. Louisiana Department of Justice, "The Final Report of the Investigation," 20, emphasis added.

7. Louisiana Department of Justice, "The Final Report of the Investigation," 20.

8. Louisiana Department of Justice, "The Final Report of the Investigation," 20.

9. Yan, Berlinger, and Robinson, "Baton Rouge Officer."

10. Mustian, "Police Records."

11. "The deity enters into philosophy," Heidegger writes, "through the perdurance of which we think at first as the approach to the active nature of the difference between Being and beings. The difference constitutes the ground plan in the structure of the essence of metaphysics. The perdurance results in and gives Being as the generative ground. This ground itself needs to be properly accounted for by that for which it accounts, that is, by the causation through the supremely original matter—and that is the cause as *causa sui*. This is the right name for the god of philosophy" (*Identity and Difference*, 71–72). I'm not particularly interested in Heidegger's ontological difference, but Salamoni's prayer is an invocation that the unmoved mover, the *causa sui*, is the very ground of his being as a police officer— and more generally as a subject. He lives from this ground. And as I will show very shortly, it is precisely this god—the one as *causa sui*—that grounds Salamoni's notion of his alleged survival.

12. See Finley and Gray, "God *Is* a White Racist."

13. See Carter, "Paratheological Blackness," for more on the relationship between blackness and ontotheology—especially as I've hinted at it here. If, as Carter tells us, blackness is "an improvisatory movement of doubleness, a fugitive announcement in and against the grain of the modern world's ontotheological investment in pure being," then one can only read Salamoni's swearing and theological justification as the enactment of this ontotheological investment. It wasn't Sterling's gun that prompted Salamoni's fear; it was his blackness—a blackness that disrupted and disturbed the centrality and primacy of Salamoni's subjectivity. This is my argument for this chapter—and it is precisely what I see occurring in and through Salamoni's own reflections regarding his actions.

14. Massumi, "The Future Birth of the Affective Fact," 56.

15. Various thinkers—many of whom are trailblazers in the black feminist theoretical tradition—have engaged with flesh as a site of violence, but also as a site of indeterminate possibility. For more on this, see Spillers, "Mama's Baby"; Weheliye, *Habeas Viscus*; and Musser, *Sensational Flesh*; Moten, "Blackness and Nothingness"; Warren, *Ontological Terror*; Rivera, *Poetics of the Flesh*; Crawley, *Blackpentecostal Breath*; Copeland, *Enfleshing Freedom*; and Turman, *Toward a Womanist Ethic of Incarnation*.

16. I'm thinking specifically of Mayra Rivera's claim that "flesh carries memories of theological passions. In Christianity, flesh evokes a creative touch, divine love, and suffering. More prominently, it alludes to sin, lust, and death" (*Poetics of the Flesh*, loc. 65).

17. See Spillers, "Mama's Baby," 66–69.

18. Spillers, "Mama's Baby," 67.

19. Merleau-Ponty, *Visible and Invisible*, 139.

20. Merleau-Ponty, *Visible and Invisible*, 139–40.

21. Spillers, "Mama's Baby," 67.

22. Dillon, *Merleau-Ponty's Ontology*, 167.

23. For more on the metaphysics of law, see the second chapter of Warren, *Ontological Terror*.

24. Baton Rouge Police Department, Internal Affairs Division, "Internal Investigation Report, No. 044-16," 16 (hereafter BRPD Internal Affairs, "Internal Investigation Report").

25. Crawley, *Blackpentecostal Breath*, 197.

26. Moten, "Blackness and Nothingness," 759.

27. Moten, "Blackness and Nothingness," 757–65, specifically.

28. Crawley, *Blackpentecostal Breath*, 140.

29. Crawley, *Blackpentecostal Breath*, 139.

30. Crawley, *Blackpentecostal Breath*, 140.

31. Moten, "Blackness and Nothingness," 769.

32. Moten, "Blackness and Nothingness," 761.

33. Moten, "Blackness and Nothingness," 769. Judith Butler claims that interpellation is "the discursive production of the social subject," and this section critiques the dynamics of interpellation by way of Sterling's speech. See Butler, *The Psychic Life of Power*, 5. She, of course, is critically reading Louis Althusser's theory of interpellation in "Ideology and Ideological State Apparatuses: Notes Toward an Investigation," which can be found in *Lenin and Philosophy*, 121–85.

34. Butler, *The Psychic Life of Power*, 131.

35. BRPD Internal Affairs, "Internal Investigation Report," 8.

36. BRPD Internal Affairs, "Internal Investigation Report," 16.

37. Spillers makes a claim about the sociopolitical dynamics of grammar throughout "Mama's Baby," and Judith Butler demonstrates that, when it comes to subjectivity, grammar is not merely grammar; the grammatical *I* has social implications. See Butler, *Senses of the Subject*, loc. 726.

38. Butler, *The Psychic Life of Power*, 108–13; Althusser, *Lenin and Philosophy*, 166–67.

39. We might read Crawley's chapter "Tongues" in *Blackpentecostal Breath* as an elaboration of flesh's speech as glossolalia.

40. BRPD Internal Affairs, "Internal Investigation Report," 41.

41. Althusser draws from Christian theology claims in "Ideology and ISAs" that one of the critical dimensions of interpellation is self-identification. Drawing from Pascal's reading of Peter's name change, Althusser suggests that "if [ideology] interpellates [subjects] in such a way that subject responds: "Yes, it really is me!" . . . if everything does happen in this way . . . we should note that all this 'procedure' to set up Christian religious subjects is dominated by a strange phenomenon: the fact that there can only be such a multitude of possible religious subjects on the absolute condition that there is a Unique, Absolute, *Other* subject." Althusser names this subject as "God," but Sterling shows otherwise (see *Lenin and Philosophy*, 178).

42. BRPD Internal Affairs, "Internal Investigation Report," 26.

43. Louis Althusser claims that the "turning" in interpellation is an enactment of consciousness. "Turning" forms the subject because turning is a self-reflexive

act; it is an act of recognition—and therefore, of consciousness. The one who turns "recognized that the hail was 'really' addressed to him [*sic*], and that 'it was *really him* who was hailed' (and not someone else)" (*Lenin and Philosophy*, 174). Butler will claim that this turning of consciousness is also an expression of conscience, that the turning is as ethical and psychoanalytic as it is social-ontological (*The Psychic Life of Power*, 113).

44. BRPD Internal Affairs, "Internal Investigation Report," 56.

45. BRPD Internal Affairs, "Internal Investigation Report," 56.

46. Louisiana Department of Justice, "The Final Report of the Investigation," 20–21.

47. BRPD Internal Affairs, "Internal Investigation Report," 44–45.

48. BRPD Internal Affairs, "Internal Investigation Report," 40.

49. BRPD Internal Affairs, "Internal Investigation Report," 59.

50. BRPD Internal Affairs, "Internal Investigation Report," 72.

51. BRPD Internal Affairs, "Internal Investigation Report," 64.

52. BRPD Internal Affairs, "Internal Investigation Report," 56.

53. Department of Justice, "Federal Officials Close Investigation into Death of Alton Sterling."

54. Department of Justice, "Federal Officials Close Investigation into Death of Alton Sterling."

55. Warren, *Ontological Terror*, 73.

56. Crawley, *Blackpentecostal Breath*, 65.

57. Crawley, *Blackpentecostal Breath*, 48.

58. Merleau-Ponty, *Visible and Invisible*, 139.

59. Husserl, *Cartesian Meditations*, 15.

60. BRPD Internal Affairs, "Internal Investigation Report," 25.

61. BRPD Internal Affairs, "Internal Investigation Report," 24.

62. BRPD Internal Affairs, "Internal Investigation Report," 16.

63. BRPD Internal Affairs, "Internal Investigation Report," 44.

64. Husserl, *Cartesian Meditations*, 19.

65. Husserl, *Cartesian Meditations*, 19.

66. Husserl, *Cartesian Meditations*, 19, emphasis added.

67. For those who are not familiar, many of Husserl's works have *introduction* floating in the titles somewhere. Though he developed an expansive philosophical program, he was nevertheless introducing phenomenology up until his final book, *The Crisis of the European Sciences and Transcendental Phenomenology*. Spillers, "Mama's Baby," 67.

68. See Heidegger's "towards-which" in *Being and Time*.

69. Levinas, *Otherwise Than Being*, 132–34.

70. BRPD Internal Affairs, "Internal Investigation Report," 35.

71. Spillers, "Mama's Baby," 67; Merleau-Ponty, *Visible and Invisible*, 146.

72. BRPD Internal Affairs, "Internal Investigation Report," 22.

73. Merleau-Ponty, *Visible and Invisible*, 137.

74. Spillers, "Mama's Baby," 67.

75. Butler, *Senses of the Subject*, 54.

76. Merleau-Ponty, *Visible and Invisible*, 134.

77. Mustian, "Police Records."

78. Butler, *Senses of the Subject*, 45.

79. Butler, *Senses of the Subject*, 54–57.

80. Butler, *Senses of the Subject*, 54.

81. Butler, *Senses of the Subject*, 54.

82. Spillers, "Mama's Baby," 67.

83. Merleau-Ponty, *Visible and Invisible*, 137.

84. Spillers, "Mama's Baby," 67.

85. Spillers, "Mama's Baby," 67.

86. I'll have more to say about the affective dimensions of compulsion in chapter 3, particularly Donovan Schaefer's discussion of it. For now, however, suffice it to say that I am ambivalent about Schaefer's discussion of affect as compulsion. Subjects may move in favor of affects, but this is because these affects satisfy the subjects—and do so as a constitutive part of this world. Schaefer suggests that the sovereign self-contained subject is a fallacy, and I, in part, agree. But I also wonder, deeply, whether this affective deconstruction of the subject also obscures the violence, steeped in affects, that satisfies subjects—and therefore compels them to continue to enact violence.

87. BRPD Internal Affairs, "Internal Investigation Report," 47.

88. BRPD Internal Affairs, "Internal Investigation Report," 72.

89. Warren, *Ontological Terror*, 22, 63–67.

90. For more on the theological relation between law and guilt, see Douglas, *Stand Your Ground*.

91. Mbembe, *Critique of Black Reason*, 39.

92. Weheliye, *Habeas Viscus*, 43.

93. Crawley, *Blackpentecostal Breath*; Sharpe, *In the Wake*; Hartman, *Wayward Lives, Beautiful Experiments*.

94. Moten, "Blackness and Nothingness," 756.

95. Morrison, *Beloved*, 102.

96. For more on expression, see Levinas, *Totality and Infinity*.

97. Morrison, *Beloved*, 102.

98. Associated Press, "Mourners at Alton Sterling's Funeral."

99. Moten, *Black and Blur*, xiii.

100. I am deeply inspired by Saidiya Hartman's work in *Wayward Lives, Beautiful Experiments*. There, she often uses the phrase "terrible beauty" as a way to describe the settings and the lives of the people she chronicles.

101. Morrison, *Beloved*, 103–4.

102. "The actual living person is not," Ronald Judy writes, "predicable of the thingness of flesh: us is not *a piece of flesh*, but rather us *is flesh*." Judy is drawing from Tom Windham's claim that "us is human flesh" to understand the relationship between personhood and embodiment. Judy continues, "Windham's person *is* in relation to his generally perceived fleshly thingness. It is not a representation of substance *for* some mind that, extricating it from the vagueness of things

(the noumenality of being) through the transcendental activity of cogitation, might claim to *see* it." I read this reading as resonating with my reading of Baby Suggs's words in the Clearing. To say "here, in this here place, we flesh" is akin to saying "us is human flesh" in the sense (and perhaps in this sense alone) that both grammatical disruptions interrupt the transcendental function of a cogitating consciousness, a normative subject. "We flesh" and "us is human flesh" elude capture. They are irreducible to the parentheses, the bracketing, that can and will follow. For more on this, see Judy's brilliant book *Sentient Flesh*, particularly 5–7.

103. Morrison, *Beloved*, 103.
104. Burling, *The Talking Ape*, 26.
105. Burling, *The Talking Ape*, 27.
106. Crawley, *Blackpentecostal Breath*, 103.
107. Evans, "I Wasn't Afraid."
108. Moten, *In the Break*, 1.
109. Evans, "I Wasn't Afraid."
110. Campt, *Listening to Images*, 51.
111. Campt, *Listening to Images*, 51
112. Campt, *Listening to Images*, 50.
113. Campt, *Listening to Images*, 50.
114. Campt, *Listening to Images*, 51.
115. Jones, "2 Years after Going Viral."
116. Brown, *The Repeating Body*.

3. "I AM IRRITATED, I REALLY AM"

1. And this is precisely what happened on March 22, 2015.
2. The majority of "Sandy Speaks" videos salute her viewers as "my beautiful kings and queens." We can question the binary gender logic she reinforces, but there was no doubt that she wanted her viewers to know they were beautiful.
3. Bland, "Sandy Speaks—March 4th 2015 (Somebody Loves You)."
4. Bland, "Sandy Speaks—April 8th 2015 (Black Lives Matter)."
5. See Johnson and Henderson, *Black Queer Studies*. And Marquis Bey argues in "The Trans*-Ness of Blackness, the Blackness of Trans*-Ness," "trans* is black and black is trans*." These formulations seek to reestablish the interconnectedness of blackness, trans*ness, and queerness as conditions of generative possibility within the context of black studies and black life more generally. I deeply, deeply regret that I cannot fully address blackqueerness, or, as E. Patrick Johnson puts it, quareness, within the context of this book. All I can do is gesture at it in this moment; I cannot do justice to the power of quare studies in this work, but please know: I recognize this limitation. And I will, as a blackqueer man myself, write about it in my next work.
6. Blackqueer people have been central to black resistance movements in the United States. Perhaps the most visible activist in this regard is Bayard Rustin, the openly gay theorist of the civil rights movement. But there were others:

Audre Lorde and James Baldwin are just two more historical names, and Patrisse Khan-Cullors, Opal Tometl, and Alicia Garza, the three blackqueer women who cofounded the BLM network, continue this tradition. Blackqueerness has always been with us. And blackqueer folx have always and already been the primary engines of resistance, black resistance.

7. Audre Lorde, "Uses of the Erotic," in *Sister Outsider*, 55.

8. Sharpe, *In the Wake*.

9. Lorde, "Uses of the Erotic," 59.

10. Donovan Schafer's *Religious Affects* argues that early treatments of affect were rightly criticized for being apolitical and solipsistic. He's right here, but, as I try to show later in this chapter, we must attend to these earlier approaches to see how they still structure religious experience.

11. Langford, "Records Show Bland Revealed Previous Suicide Attempt."

12. There are a host of stories regarding the Jackie Robinson West controversy. One of them is Castle, "Claims of Hypocrisy in the Jackie Robinson West Controversy." There are other stories, too: Grimm, "Little League World Series Scandal"; Konkol, "Jackie Robinson West Title Team"; Farrey and McDonald, "Little League Punishes Chicago Team."

13. Bland, "Sandy Speaks—April 3rd, 2015 (Good Friday Message)."

14. Lorde, "Uses of the Erotic," 54.

15. For reasons that will become clear later, I capitalize Affect as a nod to Eve Kosofsky Sedgwick and Adam Frank.

16. What remains so fascinating about Lorde's exclusion from affect studies is that she traffics in similar analyses that affect studies traffics in; she discusses (and criticizes) sensation, providing an antecedent counter to thinkers like Brian Massumi; she speaks of feeling in ways that resonate with Eve Kosofsky Sedgwick's claims in *Touching Feeling* (which, given the fact that both of them suffered and then died from breast cancer, raises possible readings); and she discusses anger as a politically useful emotion in ways that provide the jumping-off point for Sianne Ngai's analysis of "ugly feelings." And yet, with some notable exceptions (I'm thinking of Sara Ahmed here), we hear little from Lorde in affect studies. This is, however, to be expected; black feminists, from Hortense Spillers to Saidiya Hartman, have often been left out of these discourses, as if their analyses of wounding, empathy, and desire do not rise to the level of affect theory. This is not (simply) a complaint about canon; it is also a serious critique of the subfield's incapacity to learn from blackness—and therefore to continue to be hampered by its own myopia and homogeneity. If affect studies is about the capacity to affect and be affected, if it is about relations between bodies and—as Donovan Schaefer writes—the power relations instantiated/sustained therein, then affect theory's refusal to sit with these thinkers conditions its tendency to reify the very power relations it (seeks to) critique.

17. Audre Lorde, "Uses of Anger," in *Sister Outsider*.

18. Lorde, "Uses of the Erotic," 56.

19. Lorde, "Uses of the Erotic," 54.

20. As I've already noted in chapter 2, Merleau-Ponty turns to touch as the central starting point for a phenomenology of flesh. But Levinas also discusses touch in *Totality and Infinity*, where he writes, "In the carnal given to tenderness, the body quits the status of the existent" (258). The entire section titled "Phenomenology of Eros" is a meditation on the dissolution of the bounded subject in the name of caress, and, while this section provides significant generative possibilities, it must also be noted that Levinas's analysis of gender seems, well, antiquated. And perhaps Butler's meditation on touch is also useful here, as she writes, "when one touches a living and sentient being, one never touches a mass, for the moment of touch is the one in which something comes apart, mass splits, and the notion of substance does not—cannot—hold. . . . We are not speaking of masses, but of passages, division, and proximities" (*Senses of the Subject*, 54).

21. Lorde, "Uses of the Erotic," 56.

22. In "Uses of the Erotic," Lorde claims, "As a Black lesbian feminist, I have a particular feeling, knowledge, and understanding for those sisters with whom I have danced hard, played, *or even fought*" (59, emphasis added). Eros can be violent, but the focus is on how even this violence can be constructive and instructive in moving beyond the categorical violence of this world.

23. Morrison, *Beloved*, 248–49, 250.

24. Morrison, *Beloved*, 210.

25. Lorde, "Uses of the Erotic," 57.

26. Musser, "Re-membering Audre," 348.

27. Lorde, "Uses of the Erotic," 58.

28. "The [erotic] caress," Levinas writes, "consists in seizing upon nothing, in soliciting what ceaselessly escapes its form toward a future never future enough, in soliciting what slips away as though it *were not yet*." He continues, "[the erotic caress] *searches*, it forages. It is not an intentionality of disclosure but of search: a movement unto the invisible" (*Totality and Infinity*, 257–58).

29. "Touch . . . feel . . . essence" is a lyric from Musiq Soulchild's song "Love," from his album *Aijuswanaseing* (Island Def Jam Music Group, 2000).

30. Levinas, *Totality and Infinity*, 258. Again, it must be noted that Levinas's phenomenology of eros still remains burdened and marred by his own inability to think gender expansively; equating eros with the feminine in ways that are quite different than the way that Lorde does it, Levinas traffics in the language of "virginity" and "modesty," relegating the feminine to an inevitably and inescapably patriarchal plane. I turn to him, then, only to discuss his phenomenological analysis of eros as an analysis of ethical transcendence, of a transcendence that dissolves the subject in favor of hospitality toward and sociality with the Other, with others. He is discussed in service of Lorde's theorization, not in order to supplant it.

31. Levinas, *Totality and Infinity*, 258.

32. Lorde, "Uses of the Erotic," 53, 56.

33. Morrison, *Beloved*, 203.

34. Lorde, "Uses of the Erotic," 59. Levinas echoes Lorde's forward vision for a better world when he claims that the erotic caress consistently yearns for a *not yet*

that can never come, for a modality of relation that can't ever fully be incorporated into this world of categorical violence and cognitive subject formation. His refusal of the "intentionality of disclosure" foreshadows his wholesale criticism of the phenomenology of intentionality in *Otherwise Than Being*.

35. Crawley, *Blackpentecostal Breath*, 46. In speaking of black preaching, Crawley writes, "There is an excessive otherwise of breath, which enunciates itself with such vocables as 'hah' and 'tuh.' These are 'impure' appendages to words that are no less important for, no less generative of, meaning." The whole first chapter is a meditation on why black writing, black preaching, and black life are a different way of breathing, on breathing differently.

36. Crawley, *Blackpentecostal Breath*, 49.

37. It is difficult to pin down precisely where Crawley articulates these claims, as they are woven into his writing in ways that render citation next to impossible. This isn't to say that they aren't there; it is to say, however, that the whole of his first chapter in *Blackpentecostal Breath* operates as a whirlwind, spiraling back to earlier claims in such a way that his allergy to the body—and to the theological-philosophical thinking that focuses on bodies—is part of the entire first chapter. For example, his discussion of the "otherwise" doesn't include a definition—and he doesn't define "aesthetics" either. One must catch a glimpse of these concepts—if I should even call them concepts—through the writing itself. See *Blackpentecostal Breath*, chapter 1.

38. Crawley, *Blackpentecostal Breath*, 32–33.

39. See Levinas, *Otherwise Than Being*, 50.

40. Pinn, *Terror and Triumph*, 171.

41. Pinn, *Terror and Triumph*, 174.

42. I am indebted to my teacher and mentor, Niki Kasumi Clements, who, throughout the writing of this book, has carefully and lovingly read my work. Upon reading an earlier draft of this chapter, Clements framed this section as "flattening feeling into affect" as a way of articulating the pornographically affected subject's engagement with black flesh.

43. Josh Hinkle from Austin news station KXAN acquired audio of Encinia's interviews with the Texas Office of the Inspector General, from which I transcribed the sections. All transcriptions come from the audio recordings of the interviews. For more on this, see Hinkle, "Trooper Fired for Sandra Bland Arrest." The article has the audio of the interview embedded. If you'd like solely to listen to the interview, see the KXAN News Soundcloud page: https://soundcloud.com/user-43532926. It contains two interviews: one conducted three months after Bland's death in 2015, the other conducted on February 22, 2016, after Encinia was charged with perjury. I rely heavily on the first interview, of 2015, largely because the second one is a truncated version of the first.

44. Collister, "Trooper Fired for Sandra Bland Stop."

45. WFAA [an ABC News affiliate], "EDITED: Sandra Bland Traffic Stop."

46. Bauer, "Here's What Sandra Bland's Death Says." For Encinia's statement, see Graham, "A Perjury Charge for the Cop."

47. First interview transcript, Texas Office of the Inspector General.

48. For more on hunches, see Russell McCutcheon's chapter titled "I Have a Hunch" in Martin and McCutcheon, *Religious Experience*, 199–202. While I agree that we might need to "correct the over-emphasis on the cognitive content of the hunch," nevertheless I disagree with his overcorrection of the overemphasis, particularly as it relates to methodology—which is central to his overall project. He so heavily relies upon a scientific methodology that requires that our work be tested empirically, but such a move has its own ethical problems and, in a way, recapitulates the very violence that this book discusses, as the emphasis on a scientific methodology is beholden to a cognitive legacy that thinks theory as only what it sees—and therefore reifies the normativity of the normative subject who is the object of critique for this entire text. For a sustained critique of the scientific approach to religious studies, see Miller and Driscoll, *Method as Identity*.

49. First interview transcript, Texas Office of the Inspector General.

50. Hartman, *Scenes of Subjection*, 43.

51. First interview transcript, Texas Office of the Inspector General.

52. Highmore, "Bitter after Taste," 118.

53. First interview transcript, Texas Office of the Inspector General.

54. Ngai, *Ugly Feelings*, 188.

55. Ngai, *Ugly Feelings*, 207–8.

56. Lorde, "Uses of the Erotic," 58.

57. Encinia, "Affidavit and Complaint for Warrant of Arrest and Detention."

58. Encinia, "Affidavit and Complaint for Warrant of Arrest and Detention."

59. Spillers, "Mama's Baby," 67.

60. Massumi, "The Future Birth of the Affective Fact," 52–70. See also chapter 2 for a more detailed analysis of threat.

61. In "Shame in the Cybernetic Fold," Eve Kosofsky Sedgwick and Adam Frank write, "It is important that the many-valuedness of [Tomkins's] analogical system refers to *more than two* but also to *finitely many* values or dimensions . . . though, *as in any analogical representation, there may be infinite gradations along the finitely specified dimensions*" (108, emphasis added). While I still shudder at her discussion of biology—even as she acknowledges "we have no interest whatever in minimizing the continuing history of racist, sexist, homophobic, or otherwise abusive biologisms" (108)—my discussion of flesh's analog feelings here is meant to discuss its material and, I guess, in a way, its natural existence. I prefer the term *phenomenological*, but even here, we run into some problems. My point is that black flesh moves analogically, and, in so doing, discrete affects struggle to name themselves. They struggle to take primacy.

62. Discussing Ann Cvetkovitch's work, Sedgwick and Frank claim, "Perhaps most oddly for a 'theory of affect,' this one has no feelings" ("Shame in the Cybernetic Fold," 110).

63. Again, Sedgwick and Frank: "Insofar as they are 'theorized,' affects *must* turn into Affect" ("Shame in the Cybernetic Fold," 111).

64. See Sedgwick and Frank, "Shame in the Cybernetic Fold," 101–8.

65. "Virtual" is, as I read him, Massumi's name of the potentiality of affect—which is juxtaposed against the "actual." The two may mutually constitute one another, but Massumi is clear not to mix them up. See Massumi, *Parables for the Virtual*. The virtual, then, becomes eerily close to what Sedgwick and Frank caution against as an approach to theory. Critiquing the antibiologism of post-structuralist theory, they write, "[The adhesion of the biological with affect] may well be a historical development: as though some momentum of modernity (call it mono-theism? Call it the Reformation? Call it capitalist rationalization?) has so evacuated the conceptual space between 2 and infinity that it may require the inertial friction of a biologism to even suggest the possibility of reinhabiting that space" ("Shame in the Cybernetic Fold," 108). It's the monotheism that interests me here—which, metaphysically, can be translated into a monism—which, in another way, is precisely how one might read Spinoza's metaphysics—the very metaphysics upon which part of Massumi's work rests. In this regard, the virtual becomes a singular thing; either one is in the system, or one is not; actuality and potentiality may not be mutually exclusive, but, for thinkers like Massumi, it's certainly the more impor-tant of the two.

66. In *Being and Time*, Martin Heidegger describes concern as a mode of practical perception. *Dasein* is concerned when it is enacting and fulfilling its proj-ects. It's all practical; there's no room for emotions. Even his discussion of "moods" is situated in questions of *Dasein*'s orientation, *Dasein*'s situatedness in the world.

67. *Sorge*, "care," is Heidegger's way of discussing what happens when *Dasein*'s object of concern is itself.

68. And again, Sedgwick and Frank are lodestars, albeit this time with my own critical twist. They quote Silvan Tomkins as saying, "It is enjoyable to enjoy. It is exciting to be excited. It is terrorizing to be terrorized and angering to be angered. Affect is self-validating with or without any external referent" (see "Shame in the Cybernetic Fold," 99–100). Donovan Schaefer has a longer exposition of the autotelic capacities of affect in *Religious Affects*. What I seek to show here is that this autotelic function is not reducible to the affects that are named, but instead extend to the subjects for whom affects are their primary mode of intersubjective and social engagement. Such a move is dangerously close to Michel Henry's notion of auto-affection, which so heavily focuses on the incapacity of a phenomenological subject (or even time) to be affected by something outside itself. Despite his best efforts, Henry cannot help but reduce intersubjectivity to a Husserlian formulation of intersubjectivity as an "alter ego," as the space of two equal subjects whose equality comes from their phenomenological—and therefore pheno*typical*—homogeneity. Unable to abide difference, the phenomenology remains helplessly self-interested, reducing the entire world to being "for me," as Husserl says. For more on auto-affection, see Henry, *The Essence of Manifestation*, 187–92.

69. In *Parables for the Virtual*, Brian Massumi writes, "The kinds of codings, griddings, and positionings with which cultural theory has been preoccupied are no exception to the dynamic unity of feedback and feed-forward, or double-becoming. *Gender, race, and orientation* are what Ian Hacking calls 'interactive kinds': logical

categories that feed back into and transform the reality they describe." Not only does Massumi turn to the term *feedback* as his theoretical term for transformation; for this term to do its work, everything can and must be understood through feedback and feed-forward loops. Massumi's reading of "double-becoming," for example, reduces gender, race, and orientation to modalities of double-becoming— as if they are mere points on what can only be understood as a metaphysics of affect as double-becoming, as if they are not affective in different and differential ways. In this regard, race—and particularly racialized blackness—only serves to reform this world, "transforming the reality" of this normative world, but on its own terms. This is particularly evident in his chapter on Ronald Reagan in *Parables for the Virtual*; antiblack is only secondary to his affective analysis of Reagan's patterns of speech. In this regard, race—and even racism—merely feed back into what can only be understood as the more important work of virtual, political, and dynamically empirical analysis. See *Parables for the Virtual*, 11.

70. I want to be clear here: Massumi and Sedgwick are not the same. I have to stress that Massumi's work is far more cognitive and metaphysical than Sedgwick's; Sedgwick prefers phenomenological and felt approaches to affect. As she tells us in the introduction to *Touching Feeling*, "The title I've chosen for these essays, *Touching Feeling*, records the intuition that a particular intimacy seems to subsist between textures and emotions. But the same double meaning, tactile plus emotional, is already there in the single word 'touching'; equally it's internal to the word 'feeling.' I am also encouraged in this association by the dubious epithet 'touchy-feely,' with its implication that even to talk about affect virtually amounts to cutaneous contact" (17). My critique of Sedgwick's work, then, is situated squarely and solely in her deployment of Silvan Tomkins's work on affect, wherein the affects become psychological structures that exceed Freud's drives. There are many, many more moments in Sedgwick's work where the depths of feeling emerge (particularly in her meditations on Buddhism and her discussions of her own illness). Sedgwick isn't a metaphysician; she refuses to turn affect into a principle of being. Affect isn't ontotheological in her work. And it is precisely in this refusal that Sedgwick's work offers a kind of promise that Massumi's doesn't.

71. Lorde, "Uses of the Erotic," 59.

72. Spillers, "Mama's Baby," 67.

73. Schaefer makes a strong claim about the material dimensions of affective compulsion in *Religious Affects*, particularly in the chapter bearing the name "Compulsion." For Schaefer, objects—especially the ones we deem religious— compel through objects: a statue of Mary causes people to weep and mourn. Quoting Jane Bennett, Schaefer concludes that "body . . . means any material thing," and it is precisely this "thingification" with which I and other black scholars take issue. Having become things, black-flesh-turned-black-bodies has no say over whether or not it wants to compel such affects. *Things* simply become a nodal point in the causal affective nexus.

74. Weheliye, *Habeas Viscus*, 95. This particular section in the text is about Frederick Douglass's encounter with Covey, which Weheliye reads as an act of

pornotroping. The violence is intimate, sensual, and brutal—along similar lines as what happened with Encinia and Bland.

75. See Massumi, *Parables for the Virtual*, particularly the introduction.

76. In an earlier draft of this chapter, I'd decided to include two narratives that would show the virtuality of affect: the encounters between Patsey and Master Epps in Solomon Northup's *Twelve Years a Slave*, and between Harriet Jacobs and Dr. Flint in *Incidents in the Life of a Slave Girl*. What I wanted to show—and I still think it's important, which is why I include it here—is that, when black women asserted themselves, they became affective conduits, subjected to a particular form of violence. The widespread nature of these cases became part of the culture; and as such, assertive black female bodies became central to the fabric of American race and gender relations. If affects are "supple incrementalisms" that reside in "accumulative beside-ness," then irritation is definitely an affect; its effects accumulate over time, pornographically modulating bodies and producing the possibility of pornotroped violence in the process. See Gregg and Seigworth, *The Affect Theory Reader*, 2.

But, to be honest, I'm a bit exhausted with chronicling brutality. This text is already brutal enough. For my sake, then, I thought it would be best to simply announce that Encinia's treatment of Bland doesn't come from nowhere, that it is a part of a tradition in this country that has been unshakable. For the stories, see Northup, *Twelve Years a Slave*; Brent, *Incidents in the Life of a Slave Girl*, particularly 92–93.

77. First interview transcript, Texas Office of the Inspector General.

78. Many thinkers have discussed the white gaze, but perhaps Cornel West's treatment of the white gaze in *Prophesy Deliverance!* remains one of the most piercing analyses and criticisms of this kind of engagement. For West, this gaze isn't simply an aesthetic one. It is also indicative of a power relation, of the transcendental subject's inability to not be in control. The gaze is a constitutive one; it is a phenomenological one. It is the actions of a subject who is always and already trying to regain control over what it sees. See West, *Prophesy Deliverance!*, chapter 2, for more.

79. First interview transcript, Texas Office of the Inspector General.

80. Donovan Schaefer gets at some of this in his *Religious Affects*.

81. Though Russell McCutcheon and Jonathan Z. Smith have heavily and rightly critiqued the logic of the sacred as an experiential and affective category that obscures and elides the political dimensions of religion and religious experience, perhaps the most crushing philosophical blow to the affective study of religious experience was Wayne Proudfoot's seminal text bearing the same name (Proudfoot, *Religious Experience*). Nevertheless, the category of the sacred still persists in the field, particularly by historians of religion like Jeffrey Kripal and Stephen Finley. For more on this, see McCutcheon, *Manufacturing Religion*; Smith, *Map Is Not Territory*; Kripal, *Authors of the Impossible*; and Finley, *In and Out of This World*.

82. See Schleiermacher, *On Religion*; Schleiermacher, *The Christian Faith*.

83. Otto, *The Idea of the Holy*, 10.

84. First interview transcript, Texas Office of the Inspector General.

85. First interview transcript, Texas Office of the Inspector General.

86. First interview transcript, Texas Office of the Inspector General.

87. In *The Idea of the Holy*, Rudolf Otto calls religious experience a "creature-feeling," and describes it as follows: "all that this new term, 'creature-feeling' can express, is the note of submergence into nothingness before an overpowering, absolute might of some kind; whereas everything turns upon the character of this overpowering might, a character which cannot be expressed verbally, and can only be suggested indirectly through the tone and content of a man's [sic] feeling-response to it" (10). My suggestion here is that this is precisely what Encinia was feeling; Bland's recalcitrance and her assertiveness relativized his affective power and authority—which is why he stayed, why he lingered.

88. First interview transcript, Texas Office of the Inspector General.

89. First interview transcript, Texas Office of the Inspector General.

90. Otto, *The Idea of the Holy*, 10. What is crucial here is that, for Otto, the experience of the sacred robs the experiencing subject of any appropriate language for the situation. In fact, the entire first section of the book lays out why the neologisms Otto creates—"numinous," "creature-feeling"—are necessary but insufficient placeholders for this suprarational feeling that leaves the phenomenological subject bereft of any kind of intelligible communication.

91. For more on this, see Clements, *Sites of the Ascetic Self*. There, she makes a compelling case for the powerful subjective possibilities present in John Cassian's ascetic practices. I cannot say enough about how Clement's work—and her mentoring—has deeply influenced this text in general.

92. Bland, "Sandy Speaks—March 1st 2015."

93. Bland, "Sandy Speaks—March 4th 2015 (Somebody Loves You)."

CONCLUSION

1. Sharpe, *In the Wake*, 7.

2. Janet Baker, the mother of Jordan Baker, who was slain by Juventino Castro on January 26, 2014, spoke at an event my partner Andrea organized called HerStory: No Justice, No Peace (of Mind). The event was held at the Station Museum in Houston, Texas, on February 5, 2016.

3. Barajas, "Unarmed, Stopped, Chased and Shot."

4. Barajas, "Unarmed, Stopped, Chased and Shot."

5. Barajas, "Unarmed, Stopped, Chased and Shot."

6. Williams, "Lack of Videos Hampers Inquiries."

7. Turner and Richardson, "Racial Trauma Is Real."

8. Spillers, "Mama's Baby," 67. Wolf Blitzer interrogated activist DeRay Mckesson on the destruction of property after the Freddie Gray incident in Baltimore. The video can be accessed in Kulinski, "Clueless Wolf Blitzer Owned by Activist."

9. Cannon, *Black Womanist Ethics*, 143–49.

10. Moten, "The Case of Blackness," 182.

11. Lodhia, "Mother Whose Son Was Shot."

12. Clements, *Sites of the Ascetic Self*.

13. Clements, *Sites of the Ascetic Self*, 10.

14. Judy, *Sentient Flesh*. I wish I could say more about *Sentient Flesh*—because the text itself is brilliant in its intellectual depth and breadth—but a more sustained engagement with that text will have to await my next book. My point in bringing it up here is to signal where I am headed next—namely, an investigation of ethics in black.

15. Sharpe, *In the Wake*, 55.

16. Sharpe, *In the Wake*, 20.

17. Moten, "Blackness and Nothingness."

Abu-Jamal, Mumia. *Have Black Lives Ever Mattered?* San Francisco: City Lights, 2017.

Ahmed, Sara. *The Cultural Politics of Emotion.* New York: Routledge, 2004.

Ahmed, Sara. *Queer Phenomenology: Orientations, Objects, Others.* Durham, NC: Duke University Press, 2006.

Althusser, Louis. *Lenin and Philosophy and Other Essays.* Translated by Ben Brewster. New York: Monthly Review Press, 2001.

Anderson, Elisha. "Aiyana's Slaying a Slip of the Trigger? Debate Rages at Trial." *Detroit Free Press*, September 30, 2014. https://www.freep.com/story/news/local /michigan/detroit/2014/09/30/weekley-trial-testimony/16471915/.

Associated Press. "Mourners at Alton Sterling's Funeral Call for Justice in Fatal Police Shooting." *Guardian*, July 15, 2016. https://www.theguardian.com/us-news /2016/jul/15/alton-sterling-funeral-fatal-police-shooting-black-lives-matter.

Barajas, Michael. "Unarmed, Stopped, Chased and Shot: Why Was Jordan Baker 'Suspicious'?" *Houston Press*, December 3, 2015. Accessed April 3, 2017. https:// www.houstonpress.com/news/unarmed-stopped-chased-and-shot-why-was -jordan-baker-suspicious-7973311.

Baton Rouge Police Department, Internal Affairs Division. "Internal Investigation Report, No. 044-16." Filed October 25, 2016.

Bauer, Shane. "Here's What Sandra Bland's Death Says about Our Crazy Bail Bond System." *Mother Jones*, July 27, 2015. https://www.motherjones.com/politics/2015 /07/sandra-bland-bail-bond-system/.

Bennett, Joshua. *The Sobbing School.* New York: Penguin, 2016.

Bey, Marquis. "The Trans*-Ness of Blackness, the Blackness of Trans*-Ness." *Transgender Studies Quarterly* 4, no. 2 (2017): 275–95.

Blackwell, Brandon. "Lawyer Representing Tamir Rice's Family Defended Boy's Mom in Drug Trafficking Case." *Cleveland.com*, November 25, 2014. https://www .cleveland.com/metro/2014/11/lawyer_representing_tamir_rice.html.

Bland, Sandra. "Sandy Speaks—April 3rd, 2015 (Good Friday Message)." Posted on YouTube by Sandy Speaks, July 24, 2015. https://www.youtube.com/watch?v=mH _bET7weWk.

Bland, Sandra. "Sandy Speaks—March 1st 2015." Posted on YouTube by Sandy Speaks, July 24, 2015. https://www.youtube.com/watch?v=WJw3_cvrcwE.

Bland, Sandra. "Sandy Speaks—March 4th 2015 (Somebody Loves You)." Posted on YouTube by Sandy Speaks, July 24, 2015. https://www.youtube.com/watch?v=UONMFvm1JBA.

Bland, Sandra. "Sandy Speaks—April 8th 2015 (Black Lives Matter)." Posted on YouTube by Sandy Speaks, July 24, 2015. https://www.youtube.com/watch?v=UONMFvm1JBA.

Brand, Dionne. *The Blue Clerk: Ars Poetica in 59 Versos*. Durham, NC: Duke University Press, 2018.

Brent, Linda [Harriet Ann Jacobs]. *Incidents in the Life of a Slave Girl. Written by Herself*. Electronic ed. Edited by Lydia Maria Francis Child. Chapel Hill: University of North Carolina, 2003. https://docsouth.unc.edu/fpn/jacobs/jacobs.html.

Brown, Kimberly Juanita. *The Repeating Body: Slavery's Visual Resonance in the Contemporary*. Durham, NC: Duke University Press, 2015.

Bukowski, Diane. "Detroit Mourns Aiyana Jones, 7, Killed by Police." *San Francisco Bay View*, June 8, 2010. https://sfbayview.com/2010/06/detroit-mourns-aiyana-jones-7-killed-by-police/.

Burling, Robbins. *The Talking Ape: How Language Evolved*. New York: Oxford University Press, 2007.

Burns, Gus. "Aiyana Jones Trial: Questions and Inconsistencies." *Mlive*, June 14, 2013; updated January 20, 2019. https://www.mlive.com/news/detroit/2013/06/dissecting_the_aiyana_jones_ma.html.

Burns, Gus. "Detroit Police Officer Who Shot 7-Year-Old Returns to Job after Half Decade on Leave." *Mlive*, April 21, 2015. https://www.mlive.com/news/detroit/2015/04/detroit_police_officer_who_sho.html.

Burns, Gus. "How Aiyana Jones' Grandmother Didn't Help Prosecution's Case against Detroit Police Officer Joseph Weekley." *Mlive*, June 14, 2013. https://www.mlive.com/news/detroit/2013/06/how_aiyana_jones_grandmother_d.html.

Burns, Mark. "What the Police Officer Who Shot Philando Castile Said about the Shooting." *Washington Post*, June 21, 2017. https://www.washingtonpost.com/news/post-nation/wp/2017/06/21/what-the-police-officer-who-shot-philando-castile-said-about-the-shooting/.

Butler, Judith. *Bodies That Matter: On the Discursive Limits of "Sex."* New York: Routledge, 2014.

Butler, Judith. *The Psychic Life of Power: Theories in Subjection*. Palo Alto, CA: Stanford University Press, 1997.

Butler, Judith. *Senses of the Subject*. New York: Fordham University Press, 2015.

Campt, Tina M. *Listening to Images*. Durham, NC: Duke University Press, 2017.

Cannon, Katie G. *Black Womanist Ethics*. Eugene, OR: Wipf and Stock, 2006.

Carter, J. Kameron. "Paratheological Blackness." *South Atlantic Quarterly* 112, no. 4 (2013): 589–611. https://doi.org/10.1215/00382876-2345189.

Castle, George. "Claims of Hypocrisy in the Jackie Robinson West Controversy." *Bleacher Report*, February 13, 2015. https://bleacherreport.com/articles/2362111 -claims-of-hypocrisy-in-the-jackie-robinson-west-controversy.

CBS News. "Alton Sterling Shooting: Baton Rouge Police Release Bodycam Footage." Posted on YouTube by CBS News, March 30, 2018. https://www.youtube .com/watch?v=S4V6nmo-DIE&t=31s.

Chandler, Nahum Dimitri. *X: The Problem of the Negro as a Problem for Thought.* New York: Fordham University Press, 2013.

Christian, Barbara. "The Race for Theory." *Feminist Studies* 14, no. 1 (1988): 67–79. https://doi.org/10.2307/3177999.

Clements, Niki Kasumi. *Sites of the Ascetic Self: John Cassian and Christian Ethical Formation.* South Bend, IN: University of Notre Dame Press, 2020.

Collister, Brian. "Trooper Fired for Sandra Bland Stop: 'My Safety Was in Jeopardy.'" *Texas Tribune*, September 16, 2017. https://www.texastribune.org/2017 /09/16/trooper-fired-sandra-bland-stop-my-safety-was-jeopardy/.

Cone, James H. *The Cross and the Lynching Tree.* Maryknoll, NY: Orbis, 2011.

Copeland, M. Shawn. *Enfleshing Freedom.* Minneapolis: Fortress, 2010.

Crawley, Ashon T. *Blackpentecostal Breath: The Aesthetics of Possibility.* New York: Fordham University Press, 2016.

Crawley, Ashon T. "Stayed Freedom Hallelujah." In *Otherwise Worlds*, edited by Tiffany Lethabo King, Jenell Navarro, and Andrea Smith, 27–37. Durham, NC: Duke University Press, 2020.

Crenshaw, Kimberle, and Andrea Ritchie. "#SAYHERNAME." African American Policy Forum. Accessed December 1, 2021. https://www.aapf.org/sayhername.

Curran, Andrew S. *The Anatomy of Blackness: Science and Slavery in an Age of Enlightenment.* Baltimore, MD: JHU Press, 2011.

Department of Justice, Office of Public Affairs. "Federal Officials Close Investigation into Death of Alton Sterling." Press release, United States Department of Justice, May 3, 2017. https://www.justice.gov/opa/pr/federal -officials-close-investigation-death-alton-sterling.

Dewan, Shaila, and Richard A. Oppel Jr. "In Tamir Rice Case, Many Errors by Cleveland Police, Then a Fatal One." *New York Times*, January 23, 2015. https:// www.nytimes.com/2015/01/23/us/in-tamir-rice-shooting-in-cleveland-many -errors-by-police-then-a-fatal-one.html.

Dillon, Martin C. *Merleau-Ponty's Ontology.* Evanston, IL: Northwestern University Press, 1997.

Douglas, Kelly Brown. *Stand Your Ground: Black Bodies and the Justice of God.* Maryknoll, NY: Orbis, 2015.

Douglas, Kelly Brown. *What's Faith Got to Do with It? Black Bodies/Christian Souls.* Maryknoll, NY: Orbis, 2005.

Driscoll, Christopher M., and Monica R. Miller. *Method as Identity: Manufacturing Distance in the Academic Study of Religion.* Lanham, MD: Lexington, 2018.

Encinia, Brian. "Affidavit and Complaint for Warrant of Arrest and Detention in the Name and by the Authority of the State of Texas." State of Texas, County of

Waller, July 10, 2015. https://www.documentcloud.org/documents/2676622-Bland
-Pc.html#document/p1/a270274.

Estrada, Sheryl. "School District Employee Calls Tamir Rice's Mom 'Stupid B**ch.'"
DiversityInc (blog), January 13, 2016. https://www.diversityinc.com/school
-district-employee-calls-tamir-rices-mom-stupid-bch/.

Evans, Ieshia. "I Wasn't Afraid. I Took a Stand in Baton Rouge Because Enough Is
Enough." *Guardian*, July 22, 2016. https://www.theguardian.com/commentisfree
/2016/jul/22/i-wasnt-afraid-i-took-a-stand-in-baton-rouge-because-enough-is
-enough.

Fanon, Frantz. *Black Skin, White Masks*. Translated by Richard Philcox. New York:
Grove, 2008.

Fantz, Ashley, Steve Almasy, and Catherine E. Shoichet. "Tamir Rice Shooting: No
Charges for Officers." CNN, December 28, 2015. https://www.cnn.com/2015/12/28
/us/tamir-rice-shooting/index.html.

Farrey, Tom, and Joe McDonald. "Little League Punishes Chicago Team." ESPN,
February 11, 2015. https://www.espn.com/story/_/id/12308988/little-league-strips
-chicago-team-us-championship-suspends-coach.

Finley, Stephen C. *In and Out of This World: Material and Extraterrestrial Bodies in
the Nation of Islam*. Durham, NC: Duke University Press, 2022.

Finley, Stephen C., and Biko Mandela Gray. "God *Is* a White Racist: Immanent
Atheism as a Religious Response to Black Lives Matter and State-Sanctioned
Anti-Black Violence." *Journal of Africana Religions* 3, no. 4 (2015): 443–53. https://
doi.org/10.5325/jafrireli.3.4.0443.

Flynn, Sean. "How to Make a Police Shooting Disappear: The Tamir Rice Story." GQ,
July 14, 2016. https://www.gq.com/story/tamir-rice-story.

Glissant, Edouard. *Poetics of Relation*. Translated by Betsy Wing. Ann Arbor:
University of Michigan Press, 1990.

Goff, Phillip A., Matthew Jackson, Brooke Di Leone, Carmen Culotta, and Natalie
Ditomasso. "The Essence of Innocence: Consequences of Dehumanizing Black
Children." *Journal of Personality and Social Psychology* 106, no. 4 (2014): 526–45.
https://doi.org/10.1037/a0035663.

Gordon, Lewis R. "Race, Theodicy, and the Normative Emancipatory Challenges of
Blackness." *South Atlantic Quarterly* 112, no. 4 (2013): 725–36. https://doi.org/10
.1215/00382876-2345252.

Graham, David A. "A Perjury Charge for the Cop Who Pulled Over Sandra Bland."
Atlantic, January 6, 2016. https://www.theatlantic.com/national/archive/2016/01
/sandra-bland-trooper-indicted-for-perjury/422976/.

Gregg, Melissa, and Gregory J. Seigworth, eds. *The Affect Theory Reader*. Durham,
NC: Duke University Press, 2010.

Grimm, Andy. "Little League World Series Scandal Still Stings Jackie Robinson
West." *Chicago Sun-Times*, August 27, 2017. https://chicago.suntimes.com/2017
/8/28/18341862/little-league-world-series-scandal-still-stings-jackie-robinson
-west.

Hartman, Saidiya V. *Lose Your Mother: A Journey along the Atlantic Slave Route.* New York: Farrar, Straus and Giroux, 2008.

Hartman, Saidiya V. *Scenes of Subjection: Terror, Slavery, and Self-Making in Nineteenth-Century America.* New York: Oxford University Press, 1997.

Hartman, Saidiya V. *Wayward Lives, Beautiful Experiments: Intimate Histories of Riotous Black Girls, Troublesome Women, and Queer Radicals.* New York: Norton, 2019.

Hartman, Saidiya V., and Frank B. Wilderson. "The Position of the Unthought." *Qui Parle* 13, no. 2 (2003): 183–201.

Heidegger, Martin. *Being and Time.* Translated by John Macquarrie and Edward Robinson. Reprint ed. New York: Harper Perennial Modern Classics, 2008.

Heidegger, Martin. *Identity and Difference.* Translated by Joan Stambaugh. Chicago: University of Chicago Press, 2002.

Heidegger, Martin. *The Question concerning Technology, and Other Essays.* Translated by William Lovitt. New York: Harper Collins, 1982.

Henry, Michel. *The Essence of Manifestation.* Translated by Girard Etzkorn. The Hague: M. Nijhoff, 1973.

Henry, Michel. *Material Phenomenology.* Translated by Scott Davidson. New York: Fordham University Press, 2008.

Highmore, Ben. "Bitter after Taste." In *The Affect Theory Reader,* edited by Gregory Seigworth and Melissa Gregg, 118–37. Durham, NC: Duke University Press, 2010.

Hinkle, Josh. "Trooper Fired for Sandra Bland Arrest: 'My Safety Was in Jeopardy.'" KXAN *Investigates,* March 16, 2018. https://www.kxan.com/investigations/trooper-fired-for-sandra-bland-arrest-my-safety-was-in-jeopardy/.

Husserl, Edmund. *Cartesian Meditations: An Introduction to Phenomenology.* Translated by Dorion Cairns. New York: Springer, 2013.

Husserl, Edmund. *The Crisis of European Sciences and Transcendental Phenomenology: An Introduction to Phenomenological Philosophy.* Translated by David Carr. Evanston, IL: Northwestern University Press, 1970.

Husserl, Edmund. "Edmund Husserl's Ideas, Volume II." In *Collected Papers III: Studies in Phenomenological Philosophy,* translated by R. Rocjcewicz and A. Schuwer, 15–39. Phaenomenologica. Dordrecht: Springer Netherlands, 1970. https://doi.org/10.1007/978-94-015-3456-7_2.

Husserl, Edmund. *Ideas Pertaining to a Pure Phenomenology and a Phenomenological Philosophy.* Vol. 2. The Hague: Springer, 1982.

Jackson, Zakiyyah Iman. *Becoming Human: Matter and Meaning in an Antiblack World.* New York: NYU Press, 2020.

Johnson, Charles. "#Tamir Rice Mom Had Illegal Weapon Charge, Criminal Record." GotNews.com, November 28, 2014. Accessed April 3, 2017. http://gotnews.com/tamirrice-mom-illegal-weapon-charge-criminal-record/.

Johnson, E. Patrick. *No Tea, No Shade: New Writings in Black Queer Studies.* Durham, NC: Duke University Press, 2016.

Johnson, E. Patrick, and Mae G. Henderson, eds. *Black Queer Studies: A Critical Anthology*. Durham, NC: Duke University Press, 2005.

Jones, Ja'han. "2 Years after Going Viral, Ieshia Evans Reflects on Her Iconic Protest Photo." *HuffPost*, July 5, 2018. https://www.huffpost.com/entry/two -years-after-going-viral-ieshia-evans-reflects-on-her-iconic-protest-photo_n _5b3bbefde4b09e4a8b28129f.

Judy, R. A. *Sentient Flesh: Thinking in Disorder, Poiesis in Black*. Durham, NC: Duke University Press, 2020.

KapetanPingvin. "Sandra Bland Dashcam Video Released." Dailymotion. Accessed January 7, 2022. https://www.dailymotion.com/video/x2yustb.

King, Tiffany Lethabo, Jenell Navarro, and Andrea Smith, eds. *Otherwise Worlds: Against Settler Colonialism and Anti-Blackness*. Durham, NC: Duke University Press, 2020.

Koenig, Sara. "Misdemeanor, Meet Mr. Lawsuit." *Serial* (podcast), season 3, episode 3. Accessed December 1, 2021. https://serialpodcast.org/season-three/3 /misdemeanor-meet-mr-lawsuit.

Konkol, Mark. "Jackie Robinson West Title Team Only Had 5 Eligible Players: Little League." *DNAinfo*, Chicago, August 11, 2015. https://www.dnainfo.com/chicago /20150811/morgan-park/jackie-robinson-west-case-doesnt-end-before-little -league-dishes-dirt.

Kripal, Jeffrey J. *Authors of the Impossible: The Paranormal and the Sacred*. Chicago: University of Chicago Press, 2011.

Kulinski, Kyle. "Clueless Wolf Blitzer Owned by Activist." Posted on YouTube by Secular Talk, May 1, 2015. https://www.youtube.com/watch?v=x0HvohCa5ZA.

Lane, Emily. "Alton Sterling and His CD-Selling Gig Made Him a Neighborhood Fixture." *New Orleans Times-Picayune*, July 7, 2016. https://www.nola.com/news /crime_police/article_314d96b0-3b3c-5df5-a924-56a9d9769404.html.

Langford, Terri. "Records Show Bland Revealed Previous Suicide Attempt." *Texas Tribune*, July 23, 2015. https://www.texastribune.org/2015/07/22/dps-sandra-bland -video-wasnt-doctored/.

Lebron, Christopher J. *The Making of Black Lives Matter: A Brief History of an Idea*. New York: Oxford University Press, 2017.

LeDuff, Charlie. "What Killed Aiyana Stanley-Jones?" *Mother Jones* (blog), November/December 2010. https://www.motherjones.com/politics/2010/09 /aiyana-stanley-jones-detroit/.

Levinas, Emmanuel. "Enigma and Phenomenon." In *Levinas: Basic Philosophical Writings*. Bloomington: Indiana University Press, 1996.

Levinas, Emmanuel. *Otherwise Than Being, or Beyond Essence*. Translated by Alphonso Lingis. Pittsburgh: Duquesne University Press, 1998.

Levinas, Emmanuel. *Totality and Infinity: An Essay on Exteriority*. Translated by Alphonso Lingis. Pittsburgh: Duquesne University Press, 1969.

Lind, Dara. "The FBI Is Trying to Get Better Data on Police Killings. Here's What We Know Now." Vox, August 21, 2014. https://www.vox.com/2014/8/21/6051043 /how-many-people-killed-police-statistics-homicide-official-black.

Lodhia, Pooja. "Mother Whose Son Was Shot by Off-Duty HPD Officer Says Protests Bring Her Hope." *ABC13 Eyewitness News*, June 5, 2020. https://abc13.com/6233639/.

Loehmann, Timothy. "Timothy Loehmann Statement." DocumentCloud, contributed by Jaeah Lee (*Mother Jones*), November 30, 2015. https://www .documentcloud.org/documents/2631171-timothy-loehmann-statement.html.

Long, Charles. "Mircea Eliade and the Imagination of Matter." *Journal for Cultural and Religious Theory* 1, no. 2 (2000).

Long, Charles. *Significations: Signs, Symbols, and Images in the Interpretation of Religion*. Aurora, IL: Davies Group, 1995.

Lorde, Audre. *Sister Outsider: Essays and Speeches*. New York: Penguin, 2020.

Louisiana Department of Justice. "The Final Report of the Investigation and Determination of Criminal Responsibility and Use of Force by Officers Blane Salamoni and Howard Lake of the Baton Rouge Police Department in the Officer Involved Death of Alton Sterling Occurring July 5, 2016." March 27, 2018. https:// www.courthousenews.com/wp-content/uploads/2018/03/Alton-Sterling-Report.pdf.

Lowery, Wesley. "A Disproportionate Number of Black Victims in Fatal Traffic Stops." *Washington Post*, December 24, 2015. https://www.washingtonpost.com /national/a-disproportionate-number-of-black-victims-in-fatal-traffic-stops/2015 /12/24/c29717e2-a344-11e5-9c4e-be37f66848bb_story.html.

Lubrin, Canisia. "53 Acts of Living." *Blackiris*, August 12, 2020. https://www .blackiris.co/blogposts/2020/8/12/canisia-lubrin-53-acts-of-living-black-lives -matter-series.

Makalani, Minkah. "Black Lives Matter and the Limits of Formal Black Politics." *South Atlantic Quarterly* 116, no. 3 (2017): 529–52. https://doi.org/10.1215 /00382876-3961472.

Martin, Craig, and Russell T. McCutcheon, eds. *Religious Experience: A Reader*. New York: Routledge, 2014.

Massumi, Brian. "The Future Birth of the Affective Fact: The Political Ontology of Threat." In *The Affect Theory Reader*, edited by Melissa Gregg and Gregory J. Seigworth, 52–70. Durham, NC: Duke University Press, 2010.

Massumi, Brian. *Parables for the Virtual: Movement, Affect, Sensation*. Durham, NC: Duke University Press, 2002.

Mbembe, Achille. *Critique of Black Reason*. Translated by Laurent DuBois. Durham, NC: Duke University Press, 2017.

McCutcheon, Russell. "I Have a Hunch." In *Religious Experience: A Reader*, edited by Craig Martin and Russell T. McCutcheon, 199–202. New York: Routledge, 2014.

McCutcheon, Russell. *Manufacturing Religion*. New York: Oxford University Press, 2003.

Merleau-Ponty, Maurice. *Phenomenology of Perception*. Translated by Donald Landes. New York: Routledge, 2013.

Merleau-Ponty, Maurice. *The Visible and the Invisible: Followed by Working Notes*. Translated by Charles LeFort. Evanston, IL: Northwestern University Press, 1968.

Miller, Monica, and Christopher Driscoll. *Method as Identity: Manufacturing Distance in the Academic Study of Religion*. Lanham, MD: Lexington, 2020.

Morrison, Toni. *Beloved*. New York: Vintage International, 2004.

Moten, Fred. *Black and Blur*. Durham, NC: Duke University Press, 2017.

Moten, Fred. "Blackness and Nothingness (Mysticism in the Flesh)." *South Atlantic Quarterly* 112, no. 4 (2013): 737–80. https://doi.org/10.1215/00382876-2345261.

Moten, Fred. "The Case of Blackness." *Criticism* 50, no. 2 (2008): 177–218.

Moten, Fred. *In the Break: The Aesthetics of the Black Radical Tradition*. Minneapolis: University of Minnesota Press, 2003.

Musser, Amber Jamilla. "Re-membering Audre." In *No Tea, No Shade*. Durham, NC: Duke University Press, 2016.

Musser, Amber Jamilla. *Sensational Flesh: Race, Power, and Masochism*. New York: NYU Press, 2014.

Mustian, Jim. "Police Records: Salamoni Told Investigators He Was 'Mad at Sterling for Making Him Kill Him.'" *Advocate* (Baton Rouge), March 30, 2018. https://www.theadvocate.com/baton_rouge/news/alton_sterling/article_0eb9aaba-347d-11e8-bd2f-e3fd165b7b19.html.

Ngai, Sianne. *Ugly Feelings*. Cambridge, MA: Harvard University Press, 2009.

Noel, J. *Black Religion and the Imagination of Matter in the Atlantic World*. New York: Palgrave Macmillan, 2009.

Northup, Solomon. *Twelve Years a Slave: Narrative of Solomon Northup, a Citizen of New-York, Kidnapped in Washington City in 1841, and Rescued in 1853*. Electronic ed. Chapel Hill: University of North Carolina, 1997. https://docsouth.unc.edu/fpn/northup/northup.html.

Otto, Rudolf. *The Idea of the Holy*. 2nd ed. Translated by John W. Harvey. New York: Oxford University Press, 1958.

Pinn, Anthony B. *Embodiment and the New Shape of Black Theological Thought*. New York: NYU Press, 2010.

Pinn, Anthony B. *Terror and Triumph: The Nature of Black Religion*. Minneapolis: Fortress Press, 2003.

Proudfoot, Wayne. *Religious Experience*. Berkeley: University of California Press, 1987.

Ransby, Barbara. *Making All Black Lives Matter: Reimagining Freedom in the Twenty-First Century*. Oakland: University of California Press, 2018.

Rehnquist, William. Graham v. Connor, 490 U.S. 386 (1989). Accessed December 1, 2021.

Rivera, Mayra. *Poetics of the Flesh*. Durham, NC: Duke University Press, 2015.

Ross, Janelle. "Police Officers Convicted for Fatal Shootings Are the Exception, Not the Rule." NBC News, March 13, 2019. https://www.nbcnews.com/news/nbcblk/police-officers-convicted-fatal-shootings-are-exception-not-rule-n982741.

Schaefer, Donovan O. *Religious Affects: Animality, Evolution, and Power*. Durham, NC: Duke University Press, 2015.

Schleiermacher, Friedrich. *The Christian Faith*. Louisville: Westminster John Knox Press, 2016.

Schleiermacher, Friedrich. *On Religion: Speeches to Its Cultured Despisers*. Translated by Richard Crouter. New York: Cambridge University Press, 1996.

Sedgwick, Eve Kosofsky. *Touching Feeling: Affect, Pedagogy, Performativity.* Durham, NC: Duke University Press, 2003.

Sedgwick, Eve Kosofsky, and Adam Frank. "Shame in the Cybernetic Fold: Reading Silvan Tomkins." In *Touching Feeling: Affect, Pedagogy, Performativity*, by Eve Kosofsky Sedgwick, 93–121. Durham, NC: Duke University Press, 2003.

Sexton, Jared. "Unbearable Blackness." *Cultural Critique* 90 (spring 2015): 159–78. https://doi.org/10.5749/culturalcritique.90.2015.0159.

Sharpe, Christina. *In the Wake: On Blackness and Being.* Durham, NC: Duke University Press, 2016.

Smith, Jonathan Z. *Map Is Not Territory: Studies in the History of Religions.* Chicago: University of Chicago Press, 1993.

Smith, Mark M. *How Race Is Made: Slavery, Segregation, and the Senses.* Chapel Hill: University of North Carolina Press, 2006.

Smith, Mark Michael. *Sensing the Past: Seeing, Hearing, Smelling, Tasting, and Touching in History.* Berkeley: University of California Press, 2007.

Spillers, Hortense J. "Mama's Baby, Papa's Maybe: An American Grammar Book." *Diacritics* 17, no. 2 (1987): 65–81. https://doi.org/10.2307/464747.

Taylor, Keeanga-Yamahtta. *From #BlackLivesMatter to Black Liberation.* New York: Haymarket, 2016.

Thompson, Debra. "An Exoneration of Black Rage." *South Atlantic Quarterly* 116, no. 3 (2017): 457–81. https://doi.org/10.1215/00382876-3961439.

Turman, Eboni Marshall. *Toward a Womanist Ethic of Incarnation: Black Bodies, the Black Church, and the Council of Chalcedon.* New York: Palgrave Macmillan, 2013.

Turner, Erlanger A., and Jasmine Richardson. "Racial Trauma Is Real: The Impact of Police Shootings on African Americans." *Psychology Benefits Society* (blog), July 14, 2016. https://psychologybenefits.org/2016/07/14/racial-trauma-police-shootings-on-african-americans/.

Warren, Calvin L. *Ontological Terror: Blackness, Nihilism, and Emancipation.* Durham, NC: Duke University Press, 2018.

Weheliye, Alexander G. *Habeas Viscus: Racializing Assemblages, Biopolitics, and Black Feminist Theories of the Human.* Durham, NC: Duke University Press, 2014.

West, Cornel. *Prophesy Deliverance! An Afro-American Revolutionary Christianity.* Louisville: Westminster John Knox Press, 2002.

WFAA [an ABC News affiliate]. "EDITED: Sandra Bland Traffic Stop." Posted on YouTube by WFAA, May 6, 2019. https://www.youtube.com/watch?v=A7RaqqdFdY4.

Williams, Timothy. "Lack of Videos Hampers Inquiries into Houston Police Shootings." *New York Times*, February 23, 2016. https://www.nytimes.com/2016/02/24/us/lack-of-videos-hampers-inquiries-into-houston-police-shootings.html.

WXYZ-TV Detroit. "Officer on Trial: Joseph Weekley Testifies in His Own Defense." Posted on YouTube by WXYZ-TV Detroit, June 13, 2013. https://www.youtube.com/watch?v=VU4jjyJ97w4.

Yan, Holly, Joshua Berlinger, and Faith Robinson. "Baton Rouge Officer: Alton Sterling Reached for a Gun Before He Was Shot." CNN, July 13, 2016. https://www.cnn.com/2016/07/12/us/police-shootings-investigations/index.html.

Zielinski, Alex. "Protesters Shut Down Streets after Cop Who Killed 12-Year-Old Boy Goes Free." Think Progress, December 29, 2015. Accessed April 3, 2017. https://thinkprogress.org/protesters-shut-down-streets-after-cop-who-killed-12-year-old-boy-goes-free-13f1354d0226#.ylokwqvg7.

Index

eros/erotic, 87–96, 111. *See also* feelings; Lorde, Audre
ethics, 5–6, 22–24, 44, 117–20. *See also* care; love
Evans, Ieshia, 82–84
evil, 24–26, 114
excess, 25, 27, 38, 59, 64, 66, 76–77, 89, 95. *See also* black flesh; movement
experience, 7, 9, 11–13, 24–25, 27, 37, 82, 88–89, 114. *See also* religious experience

FBI, 58, 69–70
fear, 24–25, 77, 102. *See also* black flesh; feelings
feedback, 102–5, 109, 144–45n69. *See also* affect
feelings, 74–75, 87–95, 97–104, 106–7, 109–11, 145n70. *See also* affect; flesh; Lorde, Audre; pornography; religious experience; sense/sensation
Ferguson, 18, 21, 52, 82
finger, 32, 35, 49, 56. *See also* gun; Weekley, Joseph
first-person perspective, 11–13, 15–16, 22. *See also* privilege; violence
flesh, 26–27, 55, 70–71, 76–78, 83–84, 88, 110, 117, 120; and bodies, 52–53, 61–62, 73, 96, 128; and breath, 95–96; call of, 63–67, 79, 82; movement and touch, 66–70, 72–75, 80, 92–93; plasticization, 20–22, 9; unruliness, 61–63, 89; and violence, 20, 58–59, 73, 103. *See also* analog; black flesh; dehiscence; matter; Merleau-Ponty, Maurice; Spillers, Hortense; wounding
Floyd, George, 28–29
framing/enframing, 21–23, 37, 57, 129n59. *See also* plasticization; subject
fugitivity, 12, 17, 56, 127n41, 135n13
fullness, 91, 93–94. *See also* eros/erotic; feelings

Garner, Eric, 28–29
gaze, 37, 57, 84, 88, 105–6, 132n33, 146n78. *See also* pornography; subject
gender, 4, 28, 44–47, 61, 109, 141n20. *See also* black female bodies/flesh
gesture, 80–81. *See also* movement

God, 24, 26, 60, 65–66, 69
Graham v. Connor, 13, 26, 77, 126n31
grammar, 62–66, 78, 80. *See also* correction; language; violence
grief, 116–18
guilt, 21, 41–42, 64–65, 78. *See also* innocence
gun, 31–35, 39, 44–45, 56–57, 59–60, 68, 71. *See also* trigger

hailing, 63–67, 80, 82
hammers, 43–44, 47, 50
hands, 16, 33–34, 36, 53, 56, 80, 105, 117
Hartman, Saidiya, 8–9, 36–39, 40, 100, 124n20, 140n16
hearing, 38–39, 41–42, 56–58, 62–67, 84
Hegel, 23, 95
Heidegger, Martin, 4, 43, 48, 50, 103, 119, 123n4, 123n13, 124–25n25, 126n34, 129n59, 129n61, 130n66, 135n11
Henry, Michel, 37–38, 125n28
hermeneutics, 12, 64, 81
heterosexism, 86, 90
Houston, 86, 115, 118
Husserl, 10, 23, 37, 39, 71, 125n27, 126n34, 130n67

illegibility, 58, 65, 67, 79
impressions, 20–21, 23, 37–39, 41, 47. *See also* flesh; materiality; sense/sensation
innocence, 35–36, 40, 47, 50, 64–65. *See also* guilt
intelligibility, 12, 59, 64, 66–67, 73, 76, 92, 94
intentionality, 7, 12–13, 21, 23, 31, 37–39, 51, 61, 73, 90. *See also* body; reason/rationality
interpellation, 6, 63–67, 114, 136n43. *See also* black flesh
intimacy, 31, 73–78
investment, 6, 14–15, 116. *See also* attention/attentiveness
irritation, 17, 20, 88–89, 98–103, 107, 110, 146n76. *See also* affect; anger; feelings

Jackson, Zakiyyah, 20, 124n16, 128n48. *See also* plasticization

subjectivity, 4, 13, 19, 80, 96, 103, 109, 114
submission, 56, 68, 70, 83, 99, 101–2.
  See also correction; law; pinning
suffering, 8–9, 28, 74, 79, 118, 128n53.
  See also wounding

tasting, 38–39, 42. *See also* sense/sensation
terror, 9, 25, 27, 89, 103, 107, 114. *See also*
  threat
theodicy, 6, 17, 24–26, 47–49
thought, 6, 22–24, 29, 32–38, 51, 64, 74, 77,
  81, 119. *See also* subject; violence
thoughtlessness, 33–36, 38, 49, 51–53.
  See also actions
threat, 35, 59–60, 68, 102. *See also* black
  female bodies/flesh; terror
touch, 39–42, 56, 62, 73–78, 80, 91–93, 117,
  141n20, 145n70. *See also* feelings; flesh;
  violence
training, 33–34, 51, 97. *See also* police;
  thought; violence
trigger, 31–32, 35, 42, 45, 49, 56, 65, 115.
  See also gun
turning away/to, 7, 12, 16–17, 68, 136–37n43

unmoved mover, 89, 108, 114, 135n11
unthought. *See* thoughtlessness

vibration, 26–27, 63, 82–83. *See also*
  flesh
violence: antiblack, 4–5, 7–9, 118; and
  flesh, 12, 51, 109, 120; and religious
  experience, 26, 76, 95; and subjects,
  4–5, 10, 20, 48, 63, 103, 119–20; and
  thought/thinking, 20, 27, 31–36. *See also*
  abstractions; brutality; compulsion;
  God; police; religious experience
virtual, 103, 105, 144n65
voyeurism, 9, 57, 88. *See also* gaze;
  pornography
vulnerability, 73–74, 87. *See also* touch

wake work, 5, 13–14
Weekley, Joseph, 31–32, 34–35, 39–40, 42,
  44–45, 47–51, 80, 103, 120
Weheliye, Alexander, 27, 53, 77, 104,
  128n48
Wilson, Darren, 18, 21–22, 25
wounding, 20, 52, 61, 74, 76, 103, 109,
  128n53, 140n16. *See also* flesh

Yanez, Jeronimo, 35, 76
yonder, the, 52–53, 79–80, 88, 96, 110, 115

Zorge. See care